*Leaves from a*

# PRESIDENT'S
# NOTEBOOK

*Leaves from a*

# PRESIDENT'S
# NOTEBOOK

*Lessons on Life and Leadership*

THOMAS K. HEARN, JR.

PRESIDENT, WAKE FOREST UNIVERSITY

1983 - 2005

**Center for Creative Leadership**

CCL Press

One Leadership Place, Greensboro, NC 27410

© 2022 by Thomas K. Hearn III

Published 2022

**ISBN-13: 978-1-64761-075-3 (print)**

**ISBN-13: 978-1-64761-076-0 (ebook)**

**ISBN-13: 978-1-64761-077-7 (epdf)**

**CCL No. 1012**

# CONTENTS

INTRODUCTION ...9

ATHLETICS ...29

## COMMENTARIES ON LIFE ...57

## EDUCATION ...119

# INTRODUCTION

# *Introduction*

My father became president of Wake Forest University in the fall of 1983. During the twenty-two years he served the University, he gave hundreds of talks. Some were formal speeches, while many others were short welcomes or commentaries on national issues or events at the University.

While preparing for his retirement, he organized this material into a rough manuscript he entitled "Leaves from a Presidents Notebook." Unfortunately, he died before he could publish this collection. For many years, these essays lived on the floor of my study, and I struggled with what to do with them.

Dad told me later in his life that he found that audiences responded better when he shared how he felt about events rather than simply discussing the topic. Consequently, many of these essays share his reflections on some very personal events in his life, including growing up in rural Alabama, the birth and death of loved ones, and his thoughts on many of life's transitions. For someone who was more of an introvert than an extrovert, he shared a lot of himself in these pieces.

In addition to his interest in education, Dad was passionate about leadership and leadership development. He served for many years on the Board of Governors of the Center for Creative Leadership (CCL) in Greensboro, North Carolina. Several of these essays reveal his personal leadership journey and his desire to incorporate leadership development into the academic setting. All proceeds from the sale of this book will go to CCL.

I am appreciative of CCL's support in organizing and publishing this collection of my dad's essays.

THOMAS K. HEARN III

*Charlotte, North Carolina*

# Tom Hearn Reflections

My first encounter with Dr. Thomas K. Hearn was in 1992 when I interviewed for the position of Director of Athletics at Wake Forest University. He was my last interview appointment after two long days of interviews, but I was anxious to meet him as I had heard so much about him. In preparation for my interview, I researched not only Wake Forest but also Dr. Hearn, and I was fascinated by what I discovered—a fascination that only grew during our initial meeting.

It was far from the typical interview for such a position. I had prepared for the usual questions that a university president might ask... but he asked none of them! Instead, we just talked about college athletics (with no questions being asked) and Wake Forest University. I walked away from that interview not only appreciative of his time (the meeting lasted much longer than scheduled) but also totally impressed with his grasp and understanding of college athletics and its role on a university campus, especially Wake Forest. He made three things abundantly clear: he loved to win; expected to win; and was committed to winning without sacrificing the ideals, values, and standards of the university.

Over the twelve years I worked with him at Wake Forest University, my respect and admiration for him only grew. The quality I admired most about him was his sensitivity, which unfortunately many people didn't have the opportunity to experience. I first saw evidence of his care for the welfare of others during my first few months at the university when my wife, Linda, lost her father. Dr. Hearn wrote a lengthy note to her that was heart-felt, understanding, and supportive. We were overwhelmed by his tenderness.

There were many other similar moments during our time together, but the most meaningful to me occurred after Dr. Hearn had retired. He frequently swam in our indoor campus pool, which was in the building next to the one that housed my office, and he would often drop by for a visit after his swim. He would just walk in unannounced, and we would have wonderful conversations. It wasn't long after the university's basketball coach, Skip Prosser, had died unexpectedly that Dr. Hearn made one of his unannounced visits. When he entered my office and sat down, I was on the phone with a good friend, discussing Skip's death and the challenges and issues associated with his passing as well as my strong personal feelings about Skip and how much I missed him.

During most of the conversation, Tom sat, listened, and observed. After what seemed like a long time (I was struggling with my emotions during the conversation), Tom got up. I thought he was going to leave as he undoubtedly knew I was embarrassed. However, instead of leaving, he walked over to my chair, stood behind me, and rubbed my shoulders. After ending the conversation, I stood up and he gave me the biggest and strongest bear hug I had ever received.

That was the Tom Hearn I was privileged to know. The essays in this book will give you a glimpse of the truly important matters in his life: family, Wake Forest University, values, and education. He was a remarkable man, which is demonstrated in these essays and in my experiences with him. I am so fortunate to have worked with him and to have called him a friend.

RON WELLMAN

*Former Director of Athletics, Wake Forest University*

# Knowing Thomas Hearn

I was pleased when Thomas K. Hearn III asked me to participate in the selection of writings of Thomas K. Hearn Jr., President of Wake Forest University, for inclusion in this volume. I spent many years with him, and it was a delight to spend time with him again through his writings.

He said that mine was the first voice he heard from Wake Forest University, and that was true.

When Dr. James Ralph Scales retired, the chairman of the board asked me to staff the presidential search committee. There was no outside search firm, and I did the entire search in support of the committee. That also entailed calling the candidates who were asked to come for an interview. Thus, I placed a call to Thomas K. Hearn, Jr., Vice President of the University of Alabama at Birmingham.

When he came to Wake Forest, I continued as before, but after a few months he decided he wanted his counsel next door, and I left the law school duties behind and moved to Reynolda Hall, ultimately next door to the President's office. Then we were off to the races.

His was an active administration that transformed the nature of the university. It had been regarded as a regional university, but it became a national university under his leadership. That was one of his objectives, and a regular theme of many of his talks. It was also a period when educational institutions changed and moved into the growing world of regulation and legal responsibility. The combination made for interesting times.

One might think that university presidents—and university counsel—spend their time on academic matters with little contact with the world of business, but that is far from the truth. There are buildings, construction, purchasing, auditing, all normal personnel issues (plus some special to the academic world), bond issues, endowment investments, budgets, athletics, a medical school (which is a world unto itself), corporate structure, governance, and on and on. The president is involved in all of these things, and the counsel is there as well. If it works well, there is a close relationship, and ideally the work of the counsel is rarely apparent. The institution should move surely and with grace. That was our relationship. He was my senior in age—by 16 days. I came to know him very well and we developed a friendship that I forever cherish.

While reading many of his writings for this project, I often felt that I could see through what he was writing and know what he was thinking about as he wrote. (In the words of one piece, I knew more than the Sunday Tom Hearn.) Others though were a revelation, and occasionally I wished I could have read them (or heard them, as was many times the case) in real time.

Reading his essays, one will surely see his interest in leadership, something that was a driving force for him. He exemplified it and he taught it to others. After all, he was a teacher at heart. In reading the essays one will discern many other admirable traits and practices.

But I would be remiss if I did not take the opportunity to point out one character trait that one might not think about, but having it mentioned, one will see it in all he says, writes, and does in his career. Let me illustrate with a brief discussion of what surely was his most singular achievement. There have been three truly shaping events in the history of Wake Forest University: its founding, the move to Winston-Salem, and the change of its relation to the Baptist Convention. These three events have produced the school that it is today.

While Wake Forest had become a regional university, it was still closely tied to The North Carolina Baptist State Convention. In an earlier time of crisis, it had ceded the election of its trustees to the Convention. The Convention required they be residents of North Carolina and members of Baptist churches affiliated with the Convention. Many alumni and friends were thus ineligible. An uproar over a federally-financed research facility resulted in a "Covenant" relationship, under which Wake Forest could nominate an extremely limited number of trustees outside the restrictions but still elected by, and easily denied by, the Convention.

The Covenant was to be reviewed in five years, and such a time came shortly after Tom Hearn's arrival. The Convention did not want to review the agreement, but Tom Hearn insisted.

He saw that the Convention was moving in ever more restrictive directions that would impinge not only on the institution's current development but would forever restrict its future development and direction. He felt far too much of the institution's effort was expended in satisfying the Convention and that had to change.

It should be pointed out that no one can own a charitable, nonprofit organization. But having the power to select its governing body (whether they be called trustees or some other appellation) is as close as you can get.

The efforts required to bring about that change are poorly reported in the annals of the institution. One would think the Convention officials and those of Wake Forest University talked about the issue for a while and decided to go their separate ways. Not so. As Tom Hearn said, "For three years we knew what the most important thing was we had to work on each day." Negotiations were intense and frequent. A compromise was proposed, giving Wake Forest greater freedom in the selection of some of its trustees, but it was defeated on the floor of an annual Convention meeting. A more intense effort resulted, with Wake Forest unilaterally changing its bylaws about trustee selection.

Throughout, the Convention was represented by counsel, and the possibility of litigation lurked in the background. A loss would have forever put a halt to the developing institution Wake Forest was becoming. The pivotal moment came when, with the urging of two of his close advisors, Tom Hearn went to Charlotte to meet alone with William Poe, a distinguished attorney who was then President of the Convention. At the conclusion of their meeting, Poe said, "Tom, I think it is time we got a divorce." With his support, Wake Forest University could be set free. There was spirited debate at the annual Convention meeting. Perhaps in a short window of time, Wake Forest supporters were joined by those who just wanted to get rid of the problem child, resulting in a strong vote for the resolution.

Those were a hard, nerve wracking, and strenuous three years, with initial defeat and finally the gaining of freedom for Wake Forest to chart its own course and become the institution it is and is going to be. It could select its own Trustees. (And it has done extremely well in doing so.)

When Tom Hearn came to Wake Forest, he adopted it heart and soul. It was the school in his very being. He never sought to model it on any other institution but insisted Wake Forest would develop in its own way, guided by its founding principles and values. He devoted his life to its advancement.

Above all, the trait that I wish to point out about Tom Hearn was his pure and indomitable courage. He saw the challenges and the risks, and the existential threat, and he led the charge, through despair and concern, to ensure the future of Wake Forest was secure. He was a leader. Of all his fine qualities, and with all his accomplishments, I admire most of all his courage in meeting that challenge and all others.

LEON H. CORBETT, JR.

*Vice President and Counsel*
*Secretary of the Board of Trustees*
*Wake Forest University*
*Retired*

# Essay on Tom Hearn

I t is an honor to join Leon Corbett and Ron Wellman in writing a reminiscence of Dr. Thomas K. Hearn Jr., for this volume of his essays and speeches. I appreciate very much his son Tom putting these together, as they deserve to be read today and preserved for tomorrow as his legacy of leadership and wisdom.

I began my working life at Wake Forest University in 1979 and was present to welcome Dr. Hearn (as I always addressed him) when he arrived as our 12th president in 1983. I was working with Leon Corbett in the Legal Department and had taken on the task of coordinating the university's Sesquicentennial Celebration across the 1983-84 academic year. We had many events planned with our $150,000 budget, and many of them, of course, featured the president. The theme for our convocations that year was faith and reason, a subject Dr. Hearn, as it turned out, was very familiar.

"Faith and Reason," and their proper roles in the academy

were subjects on the mind of Wake Forest as it contemplated severing ties with the Baptist State Convention of North Carolina—could Wake Forest continue to be "Wake Forest" if it no longer was associated with its founding organization? It is one of my earliest memories of Dr. Hearn that he felt confident about the answer to this question. My friend and mentor Leon Corbett has written appropriately about the quest for Wake Forest to be "set free." Tom Hearn was the ideal leader to lead the transition from an organization sponsored by a religious body to one that articulated and developed its own identity, a process of becoming that continues to this day.

Dr. Hearn's decisiveness was evident early in his presidency. After the Graylyn fire occurred in June of 1980, the manor house at Graylyn and other buildings were restored, enlarged and modernized to become Graylyn International Conference Center. Dr. Hearn became president just as the conference center was opening. But another activity was going on at Graylyn in the years just preceding Dr. Hearn's arrival— the construction of a bandshell at the foot of the slope from Reynolda Road west to the driveway from Coliseum Drive. The bandshell was the result of a community effort to provide a permanent home for "Music at Sunset," a summer Sunday afternoon tradition in Winston-Salem where people with picnics and folding chairs arrayed on the hill to attend a concert by the Winston-Salem symphony. The bandshell was finished in 1980, but it was clear after the fire in the Manor House the property for Music at Sunset was incompatible long-term with the other plans for Graylyn. I remember being present for a meeting questioning whether the university should permit the concerts to continue—a vexing question after the construction of the bandshell. Our new president, unknown to the community, faced this tough decision knowing there would be certain adamant and influential critics—perhaps to become adversaries. The meeting concluded with his statement–the bandshell had to go.

Dr. Hearn maintained a vital, even scholarly, interest in leadership and the development of leaders—especially as it related to the academy and young people. He worked closely with the Center for Creative Leadership in Greensboro and often mused in the office about the ways of effective leaders. I quote here sentences from an essay he wrote entitled "Leadership":

"The first formal task of leadership in a group is to secure adequate planning….The next and equally important task of leadership is the communication of this plan to the group…. These skills of planning and communication are matters which people can learn to perform…The conclusion of most importance, however, is that leadership can be developed. It does not depend on the discovery of rare people…The teaching of leadership is, at bottom, amazingly simple and easy: people who lead must be taught to plan and communicate… Leaders are for the most part made, not born."

His focus on leadership and what could be done to teach leadership in the university setting was a precursor to the later work of Nathan Hatch and his founding of the well-respected program in Leadership and Character at Wake Forest.

Dr. Hearn was much involved in intercollegiate athletics as

president. Notably, he was a leading voice in the Atlantic Coast Conference's expansion to twelve teams. Ron Wellman said that "He has the respect of everyone. Once he verbally and emotionally supported expansion, it went much, much smoother."

Dr. Hearn also saw the need for college athletics reform given the mounting pressures to win against the landscape of ever-increasing financial implications. He was a founding member and later chair of the Knight Commission created to "lead reforms that strengthen the educational mission of college sport." (Knight Commission website) Several essays in this collection address issues in college athletics and their possible solution. Events in recent years would prove his concerns about the college game justified. He concludes in in the essay "Fans and Fanatics," "If college sports cannot be reformed by leaders of the academy, it is because these passions evoked by sports are too powerful for the university. To these ancient passions must now, of course, be added greed. Big money is at stake everywhere in college athletics. Television has changed everything in the modern world, including college games. The university is a poor match for the organized influence of the media."

I cannot say it better than William C. Friday, who attended Wake Forest in 1937 and who was president of the UNC system from 1956-1986, "I have a very deep respect for Tom Hearn....He set his sights on making a fine institution into a great national institution, and he, and Ed Wilson and others, and the faculty have achieved that. He worked very hard to make Wake Forest an academically strong and vibrant institution, and he has succeeded in a very substantial way."

Dr. Hearn's legacy of setting the university on its modern course as a great national institution is one for which Wake Foresters will always be profoundly grateful.

J. REID MORGAN

*Senior Vice President and General Counsel,*
*Wake Forest University*

# ATHLETICS

# *Amateurism in College Athletics*

There is an assumption at work in intercollegiate athletics which is the source of many of the problems that it faces, especially the temptations to violate ethical and educational principles. This assumption motivates the intercollegiate athletic establishment but remains—to my knowledge—unstated and unquestioned. I want to render the assumption explicit and question its truth.

The assumption is that college sports are in direct competition with other aspects of the entertainment industry, especially the sports entertainment industry. Therefore, the quality of the collegiate "product," its teams, is essential for the viability of the college sports enterprise in the marketplace. If the teams fielded by the universities do not compare favorably in skill and accomplishment with other athletic entertainment offerings, the spectators would select other options, TV interest would disappear, and collegiate sports would ultimately lose public appeal and financial viability. For college sports to survive, so this assumption goes, it must be professionalized.

This view of intercollegiate sports involves severe academic and financial implications for the enterprise. If the teams must excel, then players must be admitted to school to play, with diminished regard for their capacity as students. Athletic skill must outweigh academic considerations.

Scholarships and coaches must be multiplied. College football, we are told, must have a national playoff. Why? To compete with the Super Bowl and generate more money to invest in "product enhancement." There must be football practice in the spring or teams will not perform well in the fall. Since specialized skills are more rapidly acquired, there must be greater specialization on college sports teams—especially football. That means more players. Few are aware perhaps that Division IA football programs award up to eighty-five grants-in-aid plus other "walk-ons" who do not receive scholarships. The NFL rosters are only fifty-three players. Division IA programs have an army of coaches, graduate assistants, trainers, recruitment coordinators, and the like.

Recruitment, travel, administrative, and equipment costs are astronomical. Despite the popular conception that football is a cash cow, only a handful of the major football programs in the United States turn a profit. What football earns, it spends. With few exceptions, Division IA programs do not make money for the university. The imperative to sport is not economic, though a losing program can be a terrible financial drain!

The notion that the survival of intercollegiate sports depends on this kind of professionalism, that teams must be good enough to sell to entertainment consumers, is a powerful idea. I believe this idea is largely false. Let me explain why.

This assumption presumes a sophistication on the part of college sports fans that does not exist. Despite all the Monday morning quarterbacks, most of us are not knowledgeable observers of the contests we watch. We learn some lingo from the sports commentators (why is it only football defenses that get tired?), but the ability of most of us to judge good, better, and best in football or basketball is extremely limited. What matters is that the teams are evenly matched and that there is some competence in skill. The average fan does not know, to make the point, whether he or she is watching the Moscow Ballet or a good regional company dance. Moreover, they do not care. That is not the motivating interest of the supporters.

The assumption misperceives why the fans are there to support intercollegiate athletic contests. They are not there to see high-level football so much as to support their team and their school. They have not, in general, made a conscious con- sumer choice within the entertainment marketplace. Insti- tutional allegiances and loyalties explain the presence in the stands or in front of the television of a large percentage of the public. Institutional loyalty, not the quality of the level at which the contest is played, is the appeal.

With much less professionalism, there would still be winners and loyal fans to cheer their school and their team. Coaches and great players would still be public figures. There would still be huge television audiences. Intercollegiate sports rest mainly on institutional allegiance, not discriminating viewers who positively assess the level of competition. If this were true, the NFL and the NBA would be eliminating the college game. The people of Nebraska would still be there in mass on Saturday. It is their team.

At the NCAA meeting each year, awards are given to athletes whose careers 25 years out of school have brought credit to their schools, their sport, and their professions. Film clips of their quarter-century-ago performances are shown to a large luncheon audience. I am struck by the enthusiasm generated in the crowd by these exploits shown on large monitors. A great play brings a cheer! Much has happened to professionalize and improve the competitive level of collegiate sports in the last quarter century. But those fans were excited long ago about their teams and the exploits of their heroes, and that excitement is still communicated after a quarter century. All this suggests that excessive professionalism is not essential to the maintenance of the college sports system.

In the pursuit of professionalism, collegiate sports disregard other values infinitely more important to the university and to student athletes. In more cases than a few, we have sold our academic soul for a mess of professional sports pottage. Put another way, does it really matter to the public whether intercollegiate teams are more like the NFL or NBA or more like an extremely good high school team? Assuming equality between the teams and fair competition, our spectators would not know the difference. Moreover, they do not care. What they love is their school, a fair contest between equal contestants, and the game itself.

Love of college teams long preceded the grant-in-aid system. That love and loyalty was evident when student athletes did genuinely have to be students, before there were special admissions, soft curricula, and the rest of the concessions to the primary mission of the university. A high level of public interest would remain in intercollegiate sports without this excessive professionalism. We have professional sports enterprises; universities need not serve that purpose. College athletics serve many important cultural and social purposes. They bind people to their schools. They allow young people to learn the lessons of competition and teamwork. Those purposes are met without finding teams which compare athletically to the professionals. There is a single major difference between the NCAA and professionals: the university, whose role in creating our common future is sacred.

# Who's in Charge
# of College Athletics?

There is an assumption that the quick solution to the
athletic crisis in universities is the proper exercise of
presidential authority. The world needs to know that
presidential authority over athletic programs is one of the elements of the crisis. University presidents are, after all, responsible to governing boards and to trustees, who hire (and fire)
presidents and are the final authority on all matters involving
the institution.

Trustees do not always support their president. A former
president of a well-known school discovered irregularities in
his athletic program and duly reported these to the NCAA. He
was fired for his honesty by his trustees. Before that occurred,
he was in a meeting with the other presidents in his conference.
Discussing his self-reporting decision with his colleagues,

several presidents expressed disbelief. They could not possibly report irregularities in their athletic departments. They were not in charge of the athletic department and did not know what took place there. The school that fired its president for his honesty was severely sanctioned by the NCAA. The president was not in charge, and that was the problem.

In another case, a retiring president told his successor in one of those heart-to-heart talks that take place during transition that if the football program was successful, the trustees would grant the president the opportunity to do his job to build the university. If the football program is a loser, he warned, nothing else would be of interest to the board. His advice to his young successor: "Stay away from the athletic department; don't ask questions." That school, too, ended up on probation. The president was not in charge. That was the problem.

These stories are not unprecedented. Boards of trustees can exercise control of the athletic program outside the administration. The problem begins but does not end with trustee abuse. To make gifts to the athletic department tax deductible and, at public institutions, to protect such donations from state regulation and control, athletic programs establish "arms-length" foundations or clubs. These groups are essentially extensions of the athletic department. In many cases, they raise enormous sums of money. These foundations are not a legal part of the university and often the president does not serve on the board or review the operations or audits of these groups. These clubs exercise enormous influence, which is sometimes independent of the president. There is a cynical version of the Golden Rule:

"Them with the gold make the rules." When the president has no control over a substantial part of the athletic budget, abuses can occur as a result of the influence of these foundations. The president is not in charge of these funds. In many states, appointments by the governor or election by the senate are necessary to obtain coveted appointments with university boards. Concern for education and experience in matters relevant to university welfare are not requirements. These appointments generally go to large donors and political figures. Such trustees are often supporters of athletic programs. Such politically chosen trustees have direct relationships with the coaches, especially those who are themselves celebrities.

Special trustee-coach relationships bypass not merely the university president but the athletic director as well. These relationships mean that matters of interest to the coaching staff are handled directly by members of the board, bypassing the entire university administration. There was a celebrated case of a football coach hired by a trustee committee over the stated objections of the president.

None of these practices would be tolerated in other university programs. No other program is permitted to protect its budget from inspection and audit by the university. No dean or vice president would be recruited and hired absent the normal procedures of review and approval by the university administration. There is a clear need to establish control by the presidents over the entire athletic department program, budget and personnel. Trustees should not manage the athletic department. Ongoing discussions debate the need for accreditation of athletic programs, either as part of normal, regular university accreditation or as a function of the NCAA.

One object of such accreditation must be to ensure that the president, not zealous boosters or trustees, controls the athletic department. Approved procedures for the hiring of coaches and athletics staff must be a part of such requirements. Programs that do not put such procedures in place should be barred from postseason play.

The ultimate source of athletic corruption is not generally noticed. I was at my Rotary meeting while some leading citizens of my community were calling for the firing of a coach suffering through a losing season. Since this was not my coach, I listened with objectivity and even a detached amusement. Finally, I pointed out that they were the source of the corruption of collegiate athletics, a corruption they are first to complain of. They could not accept that their school was losing. Fire the coach! We must have a winning program! They could not let a game be a game. That public intolerance is the ultimate cause of the crisis. That abuse is not in the university, let alone in the president's office.

I am puzzled by the attitude, held by many otherwise thoughtful people, that "my team must never lose." Have we failed so utterly to teach our graduates what the university is for? I want to tell them, "Regardless of the score on Saturday, classes resume on Monday."

Among other things, sociobiologists study the impact of our evolutionary past on present society. Perhaps they offer us here a clue. When one early human group fought with a neighboring group, the survival of the group was at stake. In the present, when our team plays against a neighboring rival (in most respects, the schools are not at all rivals, but are cooperative academic enterprises), that clannish history overwhelms all our education and culture. We rush again to those caves of darkness of tribalism and warfare from which the university exists to liberate us. No wonder our "fight" songs are dominated with military images— "Die for dear old alma mater!"

University presidents find their efforts of to lead universities hampered by the forces and attitudes I've discussed in this essay. Put presidents in charge of athletic programs, and they will empower vital reform coalitions to gain the best of athletics and academics for students and alumni.

# Fans and Fanatics

The relationship of "fan" to "fanatic" is not mere semantics. Some large number of sports fans are fanatics. Out of that fanaticism arises many of the problems that plague sports, especially college sports. Why are fans fanatics?

A game, by its definition, has no consequences beyond itself. Betting on the outcome of playoffs may give extrinsic consequences to a contest, but they are external to the game itself. The game is the same game without the wager.

Given that the outcome of games are themselves inconsequential, where does this fanaticism originate? Friendships are lost over conflicting athletic loyalties, and families divided (I grew up in Alabama). Why do people invest so much about the outcome of something so trivial?

We obviously impart into athletic contests meanings that have origins in other human domains. There are several theories.

The attachment of ultimate meaning to ritualized ceremonies (which sporting contests are) suggests a religious origin. As the gods have been lost from the drama of modern life, it is reasonable to speculate that the intensity of religious feeling remains in our common psyche and reasserts itself elsewhere. Thus, the passion we attach to games is religious in origin.

Dr. Giamatti's elegiac study *Take Time for Paradise* suggests that the religious-like passion has another source. When we are freed from the necessities of work and survival, we enter a domain he calls "leisure," in which are performed our most characteristic human acts. These are "shared activities that have no purpose except to be themselves." This domain has cultural and communal attachments, and to such activities we attach great passion. Sport is a pursuit of leisure, and it renders us fanatics.

My own favorite among these speculations comes from my inadequate grasp of sociobiology. When an ancient human clan went to war against their neighbors, survival for all was at stake. Conflict, ritualized or real, evokes all those ancient war-like emotions. Winning this ancient contest was literally a matter of life and death. In these modern surrogates, as the saying goes, "Winning isn't everything; it's the only thing." "Die for dear old alma mater!" say the fight songs. You almost think some people would. These contests are residual combat.

If college sports cannot be reformed by leaders of the academy, it is because these passions evoked by sports are too powerful for the university. To these ancient passions must now, of course, be added greed. Big money is at stake everywhere in college athletics. Television has changed everything in the modern world, including college games. The university is a poor match for the organized influence of the media.

The university was established to manage the passionless but ultimate tasks of teaching the young and searching for truth. The structures of control in the university reflect this central mission. Those structures may well prove too fragile to deal with the passions enflamed by games. Universities manage teaching and learning well. We are no good at fanaticism and passion and money. Our managerial ideology reflects the traditions of collegiality and shared governance.

I sat high in the packed stadium at a bowl game last year. The place was filled with fanatics who had come great distances at great expense for this contest. The parking lot was filled with recreation vehicles, which seemed to me mobile temples, shrines on wheels, to the gods and heroes of the competing schools. The banners of conflict waved, and the bands blared the call to arms. The roar of the crowd was deafening. Sacramental liquors were served to intensify the experience of the conflict. Satellite dishes beamed this spectacle to millions elsewhere. It was spectacular in the literal sense. What is the university against these passions?

# The Question of Integrity in College Sports: Some Initial Thoughts

Ethical ideas and ideals reflect paradigms of social structures, methods of organization by which societies allocate duties and responsibilities so that there can be the achievement of common goals. Human beings are not self-sufficient. We cannot survive alone. We must live in groups, allocate duties and responsibilities within and among groups, and maintain the necessary degree of coherence and cooperation to make social organization possible.

The fundamental social paradigm is the family. In a family, members voluntarily work together for shared aims, willingly sacrificing personal welfare for the good of others in the family. Family members recognize the relationship between personal and group aims. Families exhibit a high degree of voluntary cooperation based on affection, and there is a "natural" ordering of authority.

Within Judeo-Christian ethics, those who believe that the basic moral imperative is to love other people reflect an ideal of social organization that has the family as its basic metaphor. There is a "family of mankind" in which we are all brothers and sisters living under the divine authority whose basic imperative is to "love one another."

A different social paradigm, also having an ancient history in human society, is the military model of organization. This alternative paradigm yields a different set of ethics. In a military organization, cohesion and cooperation are achieved not through voluntary commitment but through a strict hierarchical organization with discipline allocated according to rank. In the military structure, people are to do what they are told because they have been told to do so. Uniformity of action is based on commands from a superior officer and leaves no room for independent belief and perspective.

An army is not a family. The military metaphor of social organization and ethical behavior differs in basic ways from the system based on familial ideals. The basic difference, perhaps, is that family systems regard cooperation as the basic social necessity while the military scheme takes competition as the requirement of human organization.

Athletics in general, intercollegiate athletics especially, are ethical reflections of the military system of social organization. The metaphors of war and conflict are everywhere in sports, which glorifies competition and seeks victory over the foe in surrogate combat. The ruling principle—the organizing ideal in athletics—is victory in competitive conflict. In a family system, the ruling ideals are cooperative rather than competitive.

Our athletes wear uniforms and march onto the fields of battle accompanied by drums, waving banners, and the deafening roar of fans (remember that "fan" is short for "fanatic"). Team fight songs are ladened with the language of military conflict: "Die for dear old alma mater," they say in one set of terms or another. The aim of conflict is victory, not virtue or happiness. When the outcome of the conflict is important enough to the combatants, no rule is so important that it should not be bent or broken in the pursuit of victory. There are rules of war, of course, but the primary rule is "to the victor belong the spoils." The virtues of compassion and kindness, rooted in the family paradigm, have little place on any field of conflict. Our student athletes are soldiers on real and symbolic fields of conquest.

The concern about integrity in college athletics is at least partially a concern about the relationship between the ethics of militarism and competition on the one hand and the ethics of social cooperation on the other. We want student athletes to be individuals who are thoughtful, concerned for the welfare of others, who are ideal sons and daughters in the human family. But student athletes are socialized from their youth into a system that has different values and ideals.

When Dr. Sharon K. Stoll—professor and director of the Center for ETHICS at the University of Idaho—and her colleagues presented research that student athletes score progressively worse on various "moral IQ" tests, the reason may be frighteningly obvious. The moral tests are drawn from social and ethical values quite different from those which prevail in organized athletics. General social values that the tests measure (Kohlberg's levels of moral development) are contradicted by what the players on sports teams learn as they progress through the system of organized athletics.

For students and for coaches, the outcome of these contests is of ultimate importance. Someone gets to play, and someone doesn't. Someone gets a scholarship, and someone doesn't. Someone gets an extension of a contract or wins a conference or national title. Someone doesn't. Some very few will make literal fortunes. When the outcomes are so vital for those involved, is it right or not to bend or break the rules? The answer to that question is far from obvious, depending on which ethical system we presuppose.

There is thus a fundamental conflict in values between a set of norms drawn from the paradigm of the family and another pervasive scheme drawn from military organizations. The military model reigns in the lives of student athletes and athletic department personnel. This is not said in criticism of this model. As the Duke of Wellington said, "The Battle of Waterloo was won upon the playing fields of Eton." The military scheme would not have the power it has without a long history in human organization. Our subject presents us, however, with conceptual conflict growing from the differing values of differing social systems.

## NCAA Rules

The character of the regulations and rules of the NCAA inhibits or even forbids the development of thoughtful ethical judgment on the part of those who participate in intercollegiate athletics. In this rule-governed system, the question is seldom whether some course of conduct is good or bad for student athletes or even whether it is morally right or wrong. The NCAA environment dictates a circumstance in which the only question is, "Is this prohibited by the rules?" or, "Is it permitted by the rules?" Conformity to the rules has replaced ethical and moral judgment. I doubt that any of us have reflected seriously enough on this important matter.

The formal and literal observance of the rules has replaced ethical and moral judgment within the structure of the NCAA. The NCAA manual offers a compelling illustration of the fact that one cannot codify ethical conduct, that judgments of right and wrong cannot be specified comprehensively for any and all circumstances of conduct. When the rules so often conflict with common sense and with the welfare of student athletes, ethical judgment and decision-making must inevitably be impoverished. Ethical conduct ultimately depends upon personal integrity and character because the circumstances of the moral life cannot yield a comprehensive list of what to do and what not to do in every situation.

When the norms of permissible conduct are decided by reference to a manual—any sort of manual—then basic human ethical reflection and judgment will necessarily be lost.

My point is not to be critical of the NCAA rules. These rules exist because the competitive circumstances of intercollegiate athletics create an environment of basic distrust. In such an environment of distrust, regulations of ever more particularity and specificity are required to be certain that no one is able to gain—in a phrase we know and love—"competitive advantage." We need to ponder the moral implications of that phrase given the military metaphor that it reflects.

Rule-governed behavior is not the same as ethical behavior. Living by fixed rules is low-order behavior in the Kohlberg scheme. Living by the rules has been substituted in our athletic departments for personal integrity. When a coach devises an ingenious way of keeping the letter of a rule while violating its spirit and intent, we do not regard that conduct as evidence of a lack of personal or professional integrity. No penalties are exacted for such behavior. Everybody does it." This is exactly the outcome we can expect when rule conformity replaces personal integrity.

## Apollo Versus Dionysus

There is another reason why the issue of integrity in college sports poses such a complex question for the university community. One of the oldest debates in Western thought concerns the relative roles of reason and passion in the control of human conduct. The thoroughgoing rationalism of Plato was immediately challenged by the Aristotelian notion that the ends of conduct are set by desire or passion, and the only role of reason is the instrumental one of determining how these ends are to be achieved. The rationalist/romantic debate is profound. Each age renews this ancient dispute in its new terminology and with its new questions.

The university exists to exalt the role of reason, to discover truth, and to enable human beings to discover reasonable courses of action and to follow them. In other terms, the aim of the university is to diminish the power of passionate impulse in human life and society and to exalt the role of reason. (I say this despite the fact the social thinkers of greatest influence in our century and in our universities—Freud, Darwin, and Marx—did not believe that reason ultimately ruled in human conduct and society.)

We are perplexed and disappointed in the behavior of our students when, under the influence of the god Bacchus, they practice rituals and engage in behavior that remind us that we are the descendants of tribes and clans. What is "pagan" behavior? We want our students to be reasonable and thoughtful, to limit passion and its social influence. We believe that the habits of our students—in eating, drinking, sexual conduct—should be quite otherwise than they are. Why are we so surprised when, in the face of the threat of AIDS, our students do not practice safe sex?

Nowhere is the power of passion in human life more evident than in athletic contests. The very presence of these events in the university community is an institutional reminder of this ancient and troubling conflict between Apollo and Dionysus. Thus, the university's concern about athletics goes much deeper than the simple questions of academic standards and integrity.

It goes to the very purpose of athletic rituals in society and the power of the passions we exhibit there.

In the emotional climate of athletic contest, otherwise thoughtful people become frenzied and fanatical, screaming and acting in ways that contradict the commitments of those careful and always reasonable individuals who inhabit our classrooms and laboratories. For many people, going to our university-sponsored games provides the only experiences of ecstasy in their lives. People have license there to be—quite literally—crazy.

In this fundamental conflict, the football stadium confounds the library. The university community has the library at its center. The football stadium is at the fringe. But is it that way in human life? We are not sure, and in that uncertainty, there is fear. I have a friend who is a philosopher of substantial reputation and accomplishment. He is an utterly reasonable man. He is a baseball fan of a team whose competitive success has been, to say the least, modest. A few years ago, almost like a miracle, this team emerged as a contender for the conference title and the opportunity to play in the World Series. At the crucial game, my friend was there. The game was close, and in the late innings, the hero of the team came to bat with runners in scoring position. The chant of this player's name began and soon was echoing through the entire stadium. It was so loud that the place veritably shook with the noise and the stomping. My philosopher friend, too, was caught up in this ecstatic moment. But at that intense moment, he had a sudden and frightening thought that he repeated to himself then and later to me: "I know what it was like in the Third Reich."

In the athletic houses of our universities, we build institutional symbols that remind us of the dark and frightening passions of the soul. Our academic distrust of athletics is not because we know games are trivial and learning is ultimate. Our distrust is that in these rituals we confront powers that reason, and the life of reason, fears it cannot control. Universities are devoted to teaching and to the learning process. We manage both reasonably well. We understand the faculty. Our university leaders are largely products of the academic enterprise. It is therefore not surprising that we have managed athletics so poorly. It is a social embodiment of an alternate world view that, at one level, we do not understand. At another level, however, we do understand, and we are afraid: fanaticism, mass hysteria, violence, anarchy—these, too, are in the breast of the beast.

# COMMENTARIES
## ON LIFE

# Drug Users and Suppliers

A full-blown drug hysteria is sweeping the land. Presidential directives, media specials, and presidential candidates clamoring to be "tougher than thou" on this issue are evidence that we are suffering a national seizure. We are ready to call out the troops and declare war on drugs.

The chief irony is our anger at the peasants and drug smugglers. The suppliers are regarded especially evil. The suppliers are there, of course, because there is demand in American cities, towns, and schools. Our best antidrug campaign merely proclaims "just say no." It is a simple matter to blame the suppliers rather than to consider what might be done to alter demand.

Why do Americans use drugs? The answer at one level is simple. Why do we use alcohol? And no, it is not different. Drugs in a glass to imbibe are just the same as drugs to be snorted or injected. The difference is drug preference. People stumbling at cocktail parties wondering and worrying about whether their kids do drugs is a bitter human irony. "My drugs, our drugs, are not drugs." With massive self-deception, we locate the problem elsewhere. Students, by the way, are not deceived. Alcohol is a drug, the most serious threat to the health and well-being of our nation.

Why do we drink? The fact that others are doing so. Alcohol is ubiquitous, after all. Adults are as subject to peer pressure as kids. If you don't have a drink with the boss, what will he think? Total abstinence can be regarded as a social stigma, as evidence of social maladjustment.

There are other reasons why we drink, such as celebrating the major festivals and events in our lives. Mood-altering substances enable us to change the pace and temper of our lives, reduce stress, and lower inhibitions.

There is something more basic here, something fundamental to the human animal in all cultures and times. This vulnerable thing, the conscious "self" we are, is a frail and fragile island in a hostile universe. It lives—each moment of every day—under threat of extinction, with the knowledge that it is mortal and will be extinguished. The self is thus constantly threatened, always besieged by things promising to exterminate it. Think of what the self confronts in driving a car, a simple modern task. Each car you see is a threat, a source of anxiety. A "close call" reminds us how close that fear of extinction is.

The self, naturally enough, seeks relief from this constant state of anxiety. Changing our ordinary consciousness is one way the self's relationship to the world can be altered, suspended. Prayer, ritual, ceremonies, meditative states of all kinds have these effects as do games and other recreations. And so do mood-altering chemicals, including drugs. Drugs are the self's easiest shortcut to momentary tranquility.

Drugs play an important role in some strains of religious worship. Have you ever wondered why? It is an altered, not an ordinary, consciousness that can encounter God. The mystic traditions teach exercises aimed at self-transcendence. Before you dismiss this as wild speculation, ask yourself again: why use drugs?

The answer is not a simple self-destructive impulse, neither on your part nor on those who live from one fix to the next. The propensity to use drugs and become addicted to them is deep-seated. The identification of the problem—the basic human need to alter our tenuous grasp on the world—is a place to start. Next, let us evaluate the most pervasive, dangerous, and debilitating drug we face: alcohol.

By any measure, the most menacing, violent, and destructive drug is in your liquor cabinet. Alcohol is a killer. All of us know more than one person whose life has been lost or ruined to alcohol. What am I advocating? A return to prohibition? Have we not learned that it does not work? Prohibition makes wealthy the underworld. All too true. That sober lesson about the futility of prohibition applies to other drugs, namely street drugs. Prohibition works no better for these substances. What explains this irrationality?

The drug problem takes on a different complexion once we admit that the enemy is us—not the drug runners and pushers.

# Happiness

Books about happiness and how to achieve it line bookstore shelves. Ironically, some of those same books assert that happiness is indefinable, which places those authors in the dubious position of describing the pursuit of "something I know not what." Worse, we are all in a sorry state if one of the great aims of life, one of our inalienable rights, cannot be specified. Let me dispel this great mystery. Here is the definition. Happiness is the overall achievement of a person's reasonable desires. It is not complicated, but some clarification is in order.

"Overall achievement" needs some explaining. A baseball player cannot expect to bat a thousand. A good season is one in which the average is good, not perfect. We cannot expect to gain everything we seek to achieve. If this overall average is good, we are happy. If we fail to achieve most of our primary goals, we are unhappy.

Aristotle said that no one should be called happy until death. That is a pointed way of saying that happiness is not a momentary state of being. "One swallow does not a summer make." Having fun or being happy, as descriptive of momentary states, does not determine whether one is happy or not. Happy people have headaches and suffer from boredom. Happiness is an overall achievement, not a momentary state of feeling.

The ancient doctrine of hedonism reduces happiness to pleasure. Hedonism says that we only seek pleasure, but that is an error refuted by common sense. Some of our desires may be for pleasure, but people desire many things other than pleasure. Besides pleasure, we seek friendship, success in our endeavors, the welfare of others, and many other things.

"Reasonable desires" are important to the definition. Many people have unreasonable desires—destructive eating habits, drug addiction, and impulses to gamble to take undue risks. They may bring transitory pleasure, which is another evidence pleasure and happiness are not the same. Reasonable desires must be related realistically to our place in the world and our skills and abilities. It is unreasonable for me to desire a royal title, however much I might imagine it would bring me happiness. It would be unreasonable for me to seek to be a tennis professional because however much I love the game, I lack the requisite physical skills. There are many things that I might like, but which are not reasonable goals of my achievement. To set out to achieve the impossible Don Quixote–like "dream the impossible dream," makes better fiction than fact. Reasonable desires must offer some prospect of achievement.

Reasonable desires fall into two categories. Short-term goals are usually quite specific and have an object achievable within a specific period. These goals include finishing school, reading books, taking a trip, or seeing a movie. Long-term goals are less specific and take longer. Our personal and professional ambitions are long-term goals. Emotional and career concerns are important long-term aspirations. Desires to be successful in such undertakings stretch out over many years and change as we move through various stages of our lives.

It is important that there be convergence and consistency between our short- and long-term goals, but unfortunately there often is not. If a long-term goal requires a successful education, short-term achievements must support that ambition. People sacrifice long-term options by short-term failures. Our goals are not always what we say or believe they are. Many people say that their families are the most important element in their happiness but in fact they sacrifice their families for other outcomes that are regarded as the truly primary element.

Egoists believe that happiness is an entirely self-serving concept—that all desires are based on individual self-interest and self-satisfaction. Selfish desires, desires that improve or enhance the self, are important to everyone. However, almost all long-term objectives, especially those having to do with emotional and personal satisfactions, involve concern and care for others.

There is a great deal of popular but misguided opinion that attempts to reduce altruism and concern for others to simple self-interest. Vital life achievements seldom take place without the assistance and cooperation of others. Personal achievements involve social cohesion and the support of others. Parents, teach-ers, mentors, and helpers of all sorts cause cynical selfishness to fail in the light of common sense and ordinary experience. A scheme of desire that fails to accord place to the welfare of others is likely to be impoverished in concept and in achievement. As selves, we live in communities of other selves. That fact conditions the quest for happiness. Social beings will typically be happy in societies which offer mutual aid and comfort.

Luck, chance, or fate also plays a role in this equation. The Stoics thought happiness was entirely within the grasp of each person. Each person, according to Stoic doctrine, could master his or her own desires. If you restrict desires to the purely achievable, especially those involving your own inner life, your happiness is all but guaranteed. The Stoic program, however, is basically a counsel of despair.

We set life plans out into the world knowing that in important ways we do not control the outcomes. Fate can be harsh. It can take away those we love. Our plans can falter on political or economic turns of fortune. We are not guaranteed happiness either by the diligence of our efforts or by the kind-ness of fate. Immanuel Kant took the failure of this life to guar-antee happiness to those who deserve it as moral proof of an afterlife in which virtue and well-being would be reconciled. The rain that waters the crops of the unjust, Kant thought, could not be left as a permanent condition in a moral universe.

Happiness is the overall achievement of rational desires. This means that the specific content of happiness will differ for each person, which is what some people mean by the claim that happiness is "indefinable." We are different beings, thankfully, and differing personalities and abilities yield alternative plans for happiness. This does not mean that happiness has no definition. It is a formula into which each person pours a unique content.

This is not ideal construction. This definition is meant to reflect a practice ordinary people follow implicitly in the ordering of their lives through our complex and confusing world. One aim of philosophy and philosophers since Plato has been to enable people to examine carefully the values underlying their own experience. Reflection on the nature of happiness is meant to improve our chance to achieve that desired human achievement. Here is a reasonable theory. It is up to each of us to practice it.

# Technology and
# Social Change

As the pace of technology development increases, our record at anticipating and hence directing the social implications of technology has become a matter of serious concern. This failure has serious consequences. At worst, rather than technology serving known human social aims, just the reverse happens. Social requirements are changed to meet the demands and requirements of technology. Setting out to create a means to some end of our choosing, the technological means creates new ends that we did not intend or desire.

The most frightening example of this technological reversal is provided by the political seasons we Americans endure. One of the merits of television, we were once told, would be to improve and enhance the existing process. This then-new technology was to serve a known human purpose. People would see and hear candidates. Political education was to improve, and democracy's most significant progress was to be strengthened.

Just the reverse has happened. Far from strengthening our political system, television and the Internet have transformed the system to meet their own intrinsic requirements. Every election season, we learn we no longer have a political process. We have, to our great detriment, a media process. Candidates must speak, look, and organize their schedules to meet the requirements of the media. The candidates are presented and packaged like commodities to be marketed for media audiences. Issues are defined and discussed not from conviction or public need but as media poses designed to gain what is, in effect, a higher media market share.

This matter needs little argument. It seems obvious that television does not subsume its requirements to those of democratic political processes. Television and social media have transformed those processes into that of their own image. Media sources control and define politics. In case you doubt this, just consider what gavel to gavel coverage by television has done to political conventions. These venerable gatherings now have a single purpose: to sell the candidate and the party to television audiences. Camera angles and pretty people, not platforms and issues, dominate the scene.

Older technologies do not die when they are replaced by new, powerful rivals. They go to a kind of technological heaven, change status from necessity to luxury, and become the adornments and ornaments of privilege and wealth. Horses were once essential to agriculture and transportation. The "horsey set" now is a way to describe the upper crust. Horsepower has gone to heaven. Sailing is another obsolete technology given to the elite. Candlelight is a humbler example.

Technological changes are profound, and we may not notice those that occur over a long period of time. Southern neighborhoods flourished in the pre–air conditioning summers. We visited and were visited on the porches, which surrounded our homes. We swung and rocked, sipping tea and lemonade while the children played outdoors until our homes became tolerable indoors.

We introduced air conditioning to our great climatic relief, but the loss—which we did not take notice of at the time—was our neighborhoods. Southern homes no longer even have porches except as luxurious adornments. People are lonely who never were. Spontaneous visits are unheard of, and to drop by unannounced would be regarded in most circumstances as discourteous. "Neighbor" has lost most of its emotional reference. This is not a romantic appeal from the good old days. I love air conditioning however much I regret the destruction of our sense of community. My plea is that we know what we are doing and to whom we are doing it when we bring new technological partners to our common table.

And what of the future? When computer printouts inches high and filled with data are on my desk, I am invariably troubled. There are too much data for me to absorb. What am I to do? These powerful tools are transforming my institution's primary business: information. And as often as not, I notice that we must take our information as the devices of automation dictate. I am not free to choose what I want to know. It comes prepackaged. My needs are subtly transformed to the requirements of this awesome technology. I recall Bacon's dictum "knowledge is power." This is the technology of knowledge itself. It will have transforming effects we have not contemplated.

Are we wise enough to see that these information instruments of such awesome power are servants and not masters in this house of knowledge, the university? Or will it build new houses, not of our design, that we must inhabit to receive its gifts?

# Gratitude

I have not read any of the "one minute" self-improvement books, but in the time it takes to read this essay, I can make you a better manager. Even more, I can make you a better and more successful person and give you instant power to "win friends and influence people." This one-minute lesson works. It depends on no one other than ourselves for its achievement.

Are you ready for this transformation? This simple miracle worker is gratitude.

This is how to implement this startling and revolutionary idea as a manager: set aside some small moment each few days to pose the question, "Who has done something she or he deserves to be thanked for?" Follow that with a phone call or a note. On special occasions, perhaps you should send a token of appreciation. If you cannot think of anyone to thank on a given day, you and your organization are in serious trouble.

The most remarkable impact of this practice will be on

yourself, if you follow it sincerely for a few weeks. You will find yourself looking for positive things to praise rather than negative things to criticize. What you look for is what you will see. What you see, in turn, is what you will get. Gratitude creates the reward for which it is given. Gratitude changes the giver and the receiver.

Gratitude is miraculous in part because it is so rare. What is your own ratio of complaints to thanks? Mine is too dismal to contemplate. One of the most telling stories of the New Testament tells of ten lepers who were healed of their awful ailment. Only one of the ten came back to honor that gift with gratitude. As a child, I recalled being puzzled by this vivid story. As a man, I judge that one "thank you" in ten is a favorable ratio.

One reason for the relative absence of gratitude in organizations is that gratitude is not, strictly speaking, necessary in professional associations. Employees work for wages. They may earn bonuses for deeds well done. Relationships are defined in organizational charts, and people do their jobs. But in addition to monetary and professional rewards, personal gratitude is indispensable to a structure where people know that their deeds earn regard and respect. Gratitude oils the wheels of human interaction. People respond to appreciation and respect. You will find it easier and easier to find those who deserve thanks, and your need to crack the whip will diminish. People will work to earn gratitude. It is rare.

Gratitude transcends levels of human interaction based on duties and rights. People who do what duty requires, what they are supposed to do, are not entitled to gratitude. They have done what they should do. Gratitude is not normally a requirement. It is a gift, a grace, that transcends duty and the mutual obligations of duty. Because it may be or seem undeserved or unnecessary, gratitude is all the more prized and appreciated.

The proliferation of rights in our time may also explain the relative absence of gratitude among us. If something is due me as a matter of right, if I am entitled to it, then I have no reason to be grateful to those who give it to me. What I have a right to, you have a duty to provide. Gratitude is not part of this reciprocal relationship. Gratitude is a gift, not requirement. That is why gratitude is so compelling.

I promised a management miracle in these few words. Try gratitude. You will see that it works. This is not an exercise in calculation or control. We do not thank people to motivate effort, though it will have that effect. Gratitude is the proper response among people who are beneficiaries of mutual and reciprocal aid. Gratitude is not, thus, a lesson in management. It is a lesson in life.

# Imitations of Immortality

I am on a diet. People on diets are frightful bores because we are obsessed with food. We assume everyone wants to know how the war against fat is going.

This is partly a strategic maneuver. The diet books tell us to spread the word among friends and associates. This creates expectations in others around us, which, in turn, reinforces dietetic resolve. The dieter's motto: *Man ist, was Man isst* ("one is what one eats," from the German). What else but food is worth discussion among serious people?

My problem has a history. Some years ago, I spent the summer in Vienna. You think of Vienna as a cultural and historical center. To me, Vienna is the chocolate capital of the world. I love chocolate, and I enjoyed a particularly good time in Vienna, seeing that no delicacy went untasted.

"Eating Season," the annual celebration of gluttony, begins at Thanksgiving and goes through New Year's Day. I enjoy

Eating Season and had a particularly good season this year. At any rate, for several years I have gained a few pounds each year, a gradually growing problem. New clothes are expensive. This is to say that my diet derives from bitter necessity, which makes me unhappy with myself as well as tedious to others.

There is something more to my unease. My sense of disquiet goes further than a personal dissatisfaction. Taking care of yourself is prudent and rational. I am glad to see people on the move, doing things which maintain and preserve well-being. On our campus, the interest in exercise among faculty, students, and staff is stretching our resources to the limit. The Benson Center and the gymnasium are full of sweating bodies. The Reynolda Woods is full of joggers and walkers. Frankly, a lot of them look miserable. But this American concern about health and fitness and wellness and "being in shape" has become obsessive and troubling. I see my own concern against a disturbing social backdrop.

There is more to fat removal than big business and good health. There is a new religion in the land, a new idolatry—the worship of the body. It has its priests and priestesses who practice and supervise its rituals. It has its scribes and most certainly its Pharisees. It has its media stars that you see on TV, telling the supreme lie that exercise is fun, and you can look like those "body-sculpted" people doing aerobics on the beach.

The Pharisees are easy to spot. They are pencil thin. They nibble carrots and drink mineral water at cocktail parties. They know a lot of numbers, including cholesterol and resting and exercise pulse rates. They know about ratios of body fat and, worst of all, the number of calories in everything. Salt is a four-letter word, and sugar is something you call your daughter. Welcome to the numerology of the "religion of the bod."

It is a religion of works. It knows no grace. "No pain, no gain." Self-denial must be the rule in the presence of sweet temptation. Like most religious movements, this cult rests upon earlier tradition. The worshipers of fitness are descendants of my Alabama grandfather. Except for his ignorance about fried food (we had fried chicken every Sunday), my grandfather has become remarkably fashionable. This represents a dramatic turn of events.

My grandfather was against everything pleasurable. At the top of his list were smoking and drinking. Despite his eight children, sex was not a fit subject for discussion. There was a theory to my grandfather's point of view: The devil had played a clever trick on us all. In his guile, the devil annexed pleasure to sin so that everything pleasurable was *ipso facto* sinful. Having discovered this, my grandfather had a simple and infallible test of right and wrong, which he generously supplied to and for all of us. If it was fun and pleasurable, it was wrong.

The disciples of fitness represent a secularized, technological version of my grandfather's world view. The modern group is not in the Department of Religion but in what Wake Forest University calls the Department of Health and Sport Science. The monastic virtues of self-denial and suffering have not departed from the university; they have simply moved to another department.

I go to Health and Sport Science to be evaluated for cardiovascular fitness, diet, stress tolerance, and the like. There I am given harsh and humbling lessons in fitness virtue. Here is a telling example: After achieving full adult height, you should never gain any weight. That locates my ideal weight at about age seventeen! I have but one reaction: "All sin and fall short of the glory of God." This is a fitness version of original sin. I can never achieve the slender perfection of the true saints and thus am destined for guilt and failure along with the fat. My grandfather loved guilt.

Given my grandfather's view, we should expect that the things good in your mouth are bad for your body, and things bad in your mouth are good for your body. That is, in fact, the way it is. It ought to be that cheesecake, ice cream, and junk food should be on every diet—several servings each day. Such delights should prevent cavities for good measure. Lettuce, spinach, cauliflower, Brussel sprouts and celery—green grasses in all forms—would be forbidden from the diets of those who are health conscious. But as I said, my grandfather's religion is the fashion of the day.

This idolatry of the body reflects other trends in our culture. Technologies offer the illusion that all problems are soluble. We once said, with pride akin to that of the first inhabitants of Eden, that people who can send men to the moon can do anything. Disease, aging, and death are reduced to technological problems, waiting for the next miracle. This contains an implicit promise of physical immortality: Stay in shape! Live longer!

How much longer? A fine Alabama public health doctor of my acquaintance, Dr. Mary Tiller, used to remind me that the mortality rate of humans is one hundred percent. The cult of fitness would have us forget.

Is a longer life a good thing? There is a line in Tennyson's hymn to the human spirit "Ulysses": "As if breath were life." That is the key. The cult of fitness confuses biological life (breath) with biographical life (human life), being alive with human experience. What is valuable to us, to others, and to the world, is biography not biology. Breath is not life.

To live longer is not an unqualified good. Are those months or years gained by pain and self-denial biological or biographical? Death can be untimely and tragic. It is not always so. We should work at the task of being human, being alive to life and its possibilities. The life we have been granted has its term. The cycles of the seasons, nature's divine way of generation and regeneration, are part of human life. In the quest for a longer span of days, let us not lose the joys of those we have been given.

I've lost ten pounds. Ten more to go.

# The Business of Busyness

P olite exchanges often begin with the question "How are you?" or "How are you doing?" Among the many polite replies, there is a frequent and odd response: "I've been busy," or worse, "I've been really busy."

The first thing to note about this business of busyness is that the reply does not answer the question. "How are you doing?" does not ask "How much are you doing?" The question is about your condition, health, or well-being, not about your schedule.

It is clear that "I'm busy" does duty for "I'm fine." To be busy is to be in good condition, doing well. Being busy has thus become a virtue, an attribute to be prized and noted. The busier, the better.

Busy has thus reached an exalted new status, becoming another of those expressions that reflects merit and bestows honor. Boy Scouts of the future may have to add "busy" to the litany of virtues (which any ex-Boy Scout like me can still recite) that runs from "trustworthy" through the entire moral landscape and ends up with "reverent."

This represents enormous progress for "busy." It was once a close neighbor of other four-letter words located in negative space on the moral map. To be busy, to engage in busy work, meant that one was doing something menial or trivial. Being a "busybody" meant that one was nosy and meddlesome. Words, like people, move around, and busy has gotten a moral promotion and moved uptown.

We all know people whose business has become busyness. They are so captured by the virtue of being busy that they have no time for recreation, community service, reading, and sometimes not even their own health and well-being. They are those for whom the song "You Need to Stop to Smell the Roses" was written. These are the saints of the virtue of busyness.

Idleness has, of course, had its advocates. Long ago in 1932, Bertrand Russell wrote an essay for Harper's Magazine, "In Praise of Idleness". Wordsworth, in Book I of The Preludes asks that we seek "no record of the hours, resigned/to vacant musing, unreproved neglect of all things, and deliberate holiday." Robert Louis Stevenson wrote "An Apology for Idlers". [The Stevenson volume in the Wake Forest Library was owned by Ida A. Wilkerson. Her note at the beginning of this essay reads, "Read to me by George Lacy, January 3, 1918." Can we imagine in this day such a literary courtship?] In his essay, Stevenson recommends that we give ourselves over from time to time to "random provocations." What Stevenson and Wordsworth recommend in opposition to busyness is not, of course, that one do literally nothing. It is the necessity that one be given freedom from the tyranny of the schedule, freedom from busyness, in order to permit the mind to wander unfettered in new and unfamiliar ways and places.

There is something important here. The more demanding a responsibility one is given, the busier one becomes, the more imperative this kind of undirected reflective thought becomes. To the busiest people is given responsibility for creativity, imagination, planning, and foresight. These responsibilities, which are strategic for any organization, are rendered impossible by busyness. Thoughtful people must not be so busy for the moment that they take no thought for the tomorrows of the institutions they serve.

The same amount of time is given to each of us. We differ radically, of course, in how we manage that resource for ourselves and others. One of the busiest and most responsible people I know—he heads a very large business organization—answers his own phone at his office. He never gives the impression that he is unduly rushed. He plays tennis, reads books, and gives thoughtful attention to people. He is a hard worker who knows the virtue of idleness.

Idleness is not laziness. Creative people find contentment and reflection and inspiration in unscheduled time. Do not be taken in by the business of busyness. When next you encounter an acquaintance, think twice before you say how busy you are.

# Types of Love

A storm has taken my regular public radio station off the air for several weeks. During this interval, I have been listening to regular popular music for the first time in a good many years. This has been a troubling experience, to learn how out of touch I had become since my children left home. The names of current artists are entirely unfamiliar, though there are some stations that specialize in the "oldies," meaning, as I discovered to my dismay, the familiar tunes of the sixties and seventies.

What struck me most vividly about this listening, however, was the subject matter of the music. It has but a single subject: romantic love and its terrible complications. There have always been love songs in plentiful supply, of course. Now it seems there are only love songs.

This reflection prompted the realization that from soap operas to romance novels to popular music, the subject of love has become the dominant, if not the exclusive, interest of popular culture. It goes without saying that the popular culture is popular, meaning that almost everyone in American society is a participant. Doubtless, this reflects, in part, the opening of the subject of sexuality to this generation. Those of us who grew up prior to World War II lived in a world where the subject of sex did not exist as a public fact. In the movies, believe it or not, the bedrooms of married couples always had twin beds. There were no girlie magazines or blue movies. Now that sex is used to promote every cause and product, love has seemingly become the preoccupation of popular culture, at least as measured by our local radio menu.

This suggests to the educator in me that we would do well to ask ourselves how effective we are in presenting a real—as opposed to the popular—understanding of love and sexuality to young people. In a larger view, perhaps this matter needs to be addressed by all of us who must live in a culture so preoccupied with the subject of love. There follows here an exercise in marking the nature of eros and its near relations on our emotional map.

There are various kinds and levels of human association, all of which involve kinds and levels of love and affection. The Greeks had three words which we commonly translate as "love": *eros* is the sort of love involved in sexual bonding, *philia* is the affection that bonds friends, a brotherly love, and *agape* describes a selfless affection, one in which benevolent concern for the other is primary. In the New Testament, God's love for the world is agape as is the appropriate human affection due the Deity.

What are the differences between eros and philia, sexual love and friendship? Of course, all such labels are highly general and can scarcely describe the idiosyncratic character of any association. People make relationships, not the other way around. Glenn Gray, author of *The Warriors: Reflections on Men in Battle*, and to whom much in these remarks is owed, makes much of the phenomenon of the comradeship that occurs when people are bonded closely in the pursuit of a common objective. In war or athletic contests or theatrical performances, people experience a sense of deep involvement with others. Very few comradeships, however, survive the loss of the common objective. The bond is in the pursuit of the objective, not in the people themselves. Comradeship, then, is a temporary relationship that seldom carries over into a more permanent bond since it is called into being by forces external to the association itself.

General labels never fully describe actual concrete human associations, but the differences between and among friends, lovers, or comrades are profound and fundamental. In the popular notions of our culture, a spouse is supposed to be both lover and friend. Yet the requirements of these two relationships are profoundly disparate. Being a spouse in and of itself is a work relationship. It is task oriented. Lover and friend by contrast are not work relationships, and it is entirely possible to have friends, and certainly lovers, with whom one cannot easily function in task-oriented activities.

Friends and lovers likewise serve different roles in human bonding. Gray comments that friendship is a relationship that enhances self-awareness. Friends love each other, at least in part, because of the contribution they make to each other's autonomy and self-awareness.

*The Warriors* is sadly no longer in print. Gray, now deceased, was a wonderful man and friend. The book reflects his great qualities of mind and spirit. Friends learn about themselves and each other through processes that retain self-identity. By contrast, love seeks union with the beloved. Lovers want to lose their identity in each other, and the marriage vows speak of two being made one. Lovers lose their identity in each other. Friends keep their individuality intact.

Experiences of ecstatic union are among the most important elements of human life. Art, religion, and sexuality derive at least some of their commonalities from the role they play as vehicles for these experiences. Our normal dealings with the world are highly structured in a dualistic pattern. Our sense of self is separate entirely from the objects of our experience. In ecstasy, that structure is transcended and we are united (the word ecstasy means "in union with") with the object of the experience. It is not surprising thus that mystics use the language of sexuality to describe union with God. Sexuality is among the most powerful experiences of union that we are capable of, the most profound human expression of our need not to be alone on the tiny island universe of the self, the lonely "I." Lovers are for each other the vehicles of these experiences in which there is loss of self into an experience of the other. Whatever is the vehicle of such experiences of union becomes a sacramental object, be it a religious or sexual object.

Sexual love is thus strongly based in human desire more

so than friendship. Not only physically but psychologically, that which lovers offer each other is fundamental to human well-being. I have wondered whether it is even correct to say that sex is an appetite, like hunger or thirst. There are the fundamental differences. If hunger is not satisfied, the organism dies. To say that one will die unless lust be satisfied is one of the oldest (and least effective) "lines" a suffering lover has ever used. The fact is that the sexual impulse, if it is an appetite, cannot be lumped together with other desires with which it differs in marked and important ways.

The basis of sexual desire, of eros, is not merely an appetitive impulse. It is an emotional need that relates directly to our most important need for a sense of connectedness in the world.

Bertrand Russell said that romantic love is the most profoundly fulfilling human emotion. Probably it is not an emotion since it is a complex of emotions and attitudes in which sexual desire plays a role. It is an enormously vitalizing experience—to be in love in this sense is to be fully alive. My grandfather in a nursing home could not speak and was severely crippled by a series of strokes, but he fell in love with a lady nursing home occupant whose condition was not much better than his own. The affair, if it can be so described, was enormously valuable to him in refreshing his spirits and reviving his interest in everything in his world.

There is doubtless wisdom in the efforts of society to restrict the role of romantic love. As Russell also points out, romantic love is profoundly anarchistic. It respects no conventions or mores. Such love is its own excuse for being and need not respect any other fact in or out of the world. Such affection is essentially transient. Novelty and freshness are inherent in the phenomenon, and the virtues of familiarity, though real, are not part of romantic love. Peak experiences, as they have been described by psychologists and poets, are just that: peaks. One cannot live at such levels of intense preoccupation and distraction.

The phenomenon of temporality, while often denied by lovers in the full blush, is surely implicit in the experience. Its transience gives love its inevitable dimension of sorrow and tragedy. Love's demise is always implicit in love's drama.

In love, much is being risked. The lover puts his or her well-being in the hands of the beloved. That jeopardy is assumed from the belief that the rewards are worth the risks. But the risks are real and the rewards are, alas, temporary.

In many respects, friendship stands in marked contrast to what has been said about love. In friendship, self-identity is reserved and respected, and there is little or no risk to one's happiness or well-being. Friendship is not contingent. Friends can be lost, of course, but not without some special episode or reason. Lovers, however, part because it was "just one of those things." Changing desires and needs have scant influence upon friendship. The emotional environment of friendship thus is stable, secure, long-term, and supportive. In this absence of contingency and risk, friendship requires honesty and freedom.

Friends can reveal the warts and weaknesses that lovers hide. Love involves essentially gaming and role playing, which has no place in friendship. Friendship is a public relationship. Love is private. Friendship is inclusive. We are anxious to share

our friends, to bring friends we have into other circles of association. We want our friend A to meet friend B, and are pleased
when A and B become friends, and are disappointed if they do
not. Love, by contrast, is exclusive. The lover's attention and
affection are totalitarian in the strictest sense. It would be a
sign of immaturity to be jealous of a friend's affection for other
friends.

But it is incompatible with the lover's affection not to feel
jealous of the beloved's attention to others. Eros thus has a
destructive undertow. Friends expand one's world. Lovers seek
a private state of mutual isolation.

These figures have been deliberately drawn in contrast too
stark for real life. To repeat, people make relationships, not the
other way around. But these stereotypes seem real to me.

It might be, though, that in greater honesty and open-
ness, friendship is revealed as the more important human
relationship. It probably is the most moral human bond, but
what it possesses in purity it lacks in intensity and the depth
of involvement. Honesty is an easily overrated virtue in human
personal dealings. To the extent that a relationship is lacking in
the guiles and ploys and games which characterize love, it lacks
dimensions of interest and richness. I want to say that friendship, through honesty, loses joy. Joy is surely as vital a matter as
honesty.

Friendship is as well a more rational matter. Friends can
explain what it is that attracts them to each other. Eros attracts
for reasons we often are unable to articulate, and even the effort
to explain "what you see in so and so" is apt to be met with

resistance. Eros arises where it should not for reasons no one can understand. As the stories of Heloise and Abelard indicate, eros has a rich history of transcending every barrier that can be constructed in human convention, law, race, or institution. Love is not irrational so much as it is arational. As Blaise Pascal said, "The heart has its reasons of which reason knows nothing of."

Here then is a brief description of the differences between love and friendship, eros and philia. For a variety of reasons (the profundity of the subject and the brevity of human life), this essay has neither conclusion nor end. I simply wish there were more songs in the top forty celebrating the joys of friendship.

# Reflections on a Childhood
# in Another Century

*My contemporaries were all brought up in some*
*degree of the nineteenth century,*
*since the twentieth did not begin till 1945.*
*That is why we are on the rack, forced into*
*one of the longest and most abrupt cultural*
*stretches in the history of mankind. Already*
*what I was before the Second World War seems*
*far more than four decades away; much more*
*like the same number of centuries.*

JOHN FOWLES, *DANIEL MARTIN*

When I first read this paragraph some years ago, these remarks struck me with the force of an illumination about my own life. Before 1945, before the nuclear age, before the end of World War II, we lived in a different century. Those of us born in that time "before the war," as we once said, have been ill prepared for the twentieth century. In historical time, this is the recent past. In cultural time, as Fowles said, it is measured in centuries.

What seems clear about a nineteenth century upbringing was that parents expected the lives of their children to unfold according to the pattern of their own lives. The parents' experience was normative for the child. For most or even all human history, the presumption of child rearing has been that children should be prepared to live as their parents and theirs before had lived. Social and institutional stability, not change, have been the presumption of the methods of teaching the young. Whatever was new or different was dangerous. Not so in the post-1945 twentieth century. Beginning with the upheavals of World War II, change rather than permanence became the presumption of our social order. We no longer expect the lives of our children to mirror our experience. They are to be prepared for change. New technologies, new professions, new places, and new requirements have become our standard expectations. Experience, rooted in permanent social expectations of the past, has no relationship to the lives we anticipate for our children. Their world will not be ours.

Something even more fundamental has happened. Reflecting on my own childhood in the nineteenth century, even the conception of the child has changed. My grandparents ran a boarding house that also served as a lunch time (we called it "dinner") restaurant in our Alabama hometown. Local businesspeople would come for lunch and close shop to do so. My grandmother's kitchen did not have electricity, and it was my job to keep her stove wood box full. You know the saying, "If you cannot stand the heat, get out of the kitchen." You had to live in the nineteenth century to know what it means. In the summer, before air conditioning, that kitchen was the hottest place on earth. My grandmother managed to stay there, hour after hour, to cook for the boarders and all of us.

When meals were served, the boarders ate first. They were the paying customers. Then, the adults in the family ate. There were lots of them. My grandmother had eight children. Last of all, the children ate. It is no accident that my favorite piece of chicken is the liver. It was usually what was left. Consider this: the adults ate first, and the children got the leftovers. How bizarre that seems to me now. My grandfather said (and meant): "Children are to be seen and not heard." Parents who acted in that nineteenth century way would now be regarded as insensitive or cruel. Hungry children were made to wait until their parents have eaten their fill. That sounds barbaric to the modern consciousness. Often there was no dessert left. The adults had seconds, and the children went without. No one was insensitive or cruel. Children were simply different animals then. The needs of children were not naturally and universally placed first.

The revolutionary here is Benjamin Spock, who can arguably be named among the most influential persons of this century. More than 50 million copies of his book, *The Common*

*Sense Book of Baby and Child Care*, have been sold. He taught us that the needs of the children were to be put first. By the time that my own children gathered at that same dining-room table, they ate first and—no surprise—had first choice of the chicken. Spock said that the needs and the desires of children should be primary in families. I kept on eating livers until warned off by learning about cholesterol.

The word "teenager" did not exist until after World War II. In some sense, the animal did not exist either. Madison Avenue discovered that children, in their new positions of familial power, could direct family spending. After the war, the GI bill sent the Veterans to college. They did not return to the small towns and farms. They lived in a new century. My mother still lives in that former boarding house, but no other relative of that large extended family is in the county. The world that house contained is longer ago in culture than in time.

Herein lies our dilemma. In the twentieth century, the lives of the parents are only marginally relevant to the future of their children. I can still recall the expression on my children's faces when I was foolish enough to remark, "When I was your age…" They and I knew that my experience was irrelevant and unrelated. I grew up in a world where there was no television. Rhett Butler's "Damn" made *Gone with the Wind* questionable entertainment for children. My grandparents lived across the street from my great-grandparents. We did not own a car. That world seems longer ago than my own childhood. No wonder the times seem out of joint. Perhaps we can go beyond Fowles' thesis: until 1945, there were no children.

# The Most Disturbing
# Fact I Know

The obvious and fundamental things in life are hard to figure out. They are so taken for granted that, like the air, they pass unnoticed. I have just discovered such an obvious item of experience. It is also a profoundly disturbing fact. The most disturbing fact I know is that advertising works. That seems obvious now. If it did not work, there would be much less of it.

The next consideration is far from obvious and has to do with happiness. Happiness means, by definition, the satisfaction of desires. Unhappiness, by contrast, is the frustration of desire. The very purpose of advertising, of course, is to create desire, an objective it well achieves. Since most of the desires aroused by advertising go unfulfilled—thus these desires are frustrated—advertising is a source of great unhappiness in the modern world.

In an earlier, simpler age, this dissatisfaction was perhaps a matter of little consequence. The resources available to advertisers were modest and their effect on human attitudes and society were modest. But in the last quarter century, advertising has been given a powerful, new medium—television. The effectiveness of advertising has multiplied many fold, as has its effect on our desires. In short, television advertising makes people dissatisfied and contributes to social alienation and unrest. This is the most disturbing fact I know.

I sit in front of my television. I am told what sort of home I should live in, what sort of car I should drive, what sort of vacations I should take, what sort of clothes I should wear, what elegant stores I should shop in, what sort of credit cards I should use, and what sort of things I should eat and drink. These advertisements work, and I am left with many urgings.

In the average American household, the television is on a frightening amount of the time. Children, as well as adults, are being constantly told the respects in which their lives are incomplete. The lives described on television ads bear scant resemblance to their actual circumstances. People are left frustrated and unhappy by the actual circumstances of their lives.

There is further a not very subtle message that these visions of the good life are yours by right. This is the American dream. The world depicted on television is the world that should be yours. If it is not (and it never is), there is reason for anger, alienation, and protest. If the world of the ads is yours by right, someone is depriving you of something you have a right to.

I lived in the world before television. One of the people I loved best as a child was an uncle who was poor. He had little education, and over his life engaged in a series of failing enterprises. He never flew in an airplane. He saw the ocean just once, on the only vacation he ever had. He never owned a record player. His life bore almost no relationship to the visions that unfold on television. His wants and his needs were in close proximity. He was a happy and loving man. He was not angry or frustrated, and I did not believe anyone owed him anything.

Are lives like those of my Uncle B any longer possible? Are our desires so shaped by advertisers that Uncle B would have felt that someone, probably someone in Washington, had cheated him of something he deserved and was not given?

No society can offer its citizens visions of a utopia of plenty for all—yet that is just the message entering our homes for hours each night. This is the most disturbing fact I know.

# The Sounds of Silence

Some of you will recall this title from the Simon and Garfunkel album. Like many of their titles and songs, there is something enigmatic and paradoxical about the phrase. Silence has no sound, or so I once thought.

This title now has a quite literal meaning for me. Silence *does* have a sound. I suffer from an affliction called tinnitus, ringing in the ears. I am not alone. By some estimates, over 30 million Americans have this condition. For some, it is a mild annoyance, but for others it is an awful distraction, making it impossible for them to concentrate or to sleep. I am somewhere in the middle—I no longer require "masking noises" at night to sleep, though I used them for a number of years.

However annoying, tinnitus is not a fatal condition. It just drives folks crazy! Because it is not in the category of "serious" maladies, medicine knows little about tinnitus and evidently spends little effort or energy on research or treatment. "No cause, no cure," my doctor told me. Caffeine, alcohol, and aspirin can make it worse, so patients are advised to reduce their intake. Oh yes, stress also plays a role—stress, I am convinced, is the last refuge of medical ignorance. Whatever is wrong with you for which your doctor has no explanation or remedy is caused by stress. And, as the comic line goes, "Reality is the primary cause of stress."

Since I am not to be cured of this condition, I must learn to live with it. That means, in my case, avoiding the cold, especially cold wind, which can cause pain in my ears and leave my tinnitus sometimes literally whistling. So, I wear earmuffs more than most people my age. Loud noises of any kind—from the 1812 Overture to basketball games—must be guarded against. Sometimes I wear ear plugs, but for most such occasions I have decided simply to live with the discomfort until it becomes more than that. When Wake Forest University beat Carolina last year—I sat next to the student section—the joy was worth the pain.

Most of all, I miss silence—blissful, perfect, profound silence. The missing is like being young and homesick. When I was a child, I would, on occasion, crawl into a closet and seek to hold off the raucous, busy world. I wanted no sound, no light, no other external stimuli. There was something fascinating and powerful about these retreats. I remember they required a certain bravery, but what I remember best is that the silence was profound.

I do not retreat to closets anymore. Heaven knows, I would if I could find true silence there. But always when I seek the silence of meditation, my inner noise is with me. So, I live a noisy life. Often, I provide myself some kind of background sound to muffle the high-pitched ringing. My silence has a sound, an unpleasant one, and I miss the serenity, the sound-lessness of silence.

Nothing so marks for me the difference between my generation and the young people of today than the attitude toward noise. When my children were teenagers, there were no family conflicts as persistent as those having to do with when noise (i.e., music) should be permitted and how loud it should be.

I shall never forget the moment I experienced this new music firsthand. In quite ancient times, student parties were "chaperoned." Isn't it a quaint word as well as a quaint idea? As a young professor at William and Mary, I showed up as requested by the students and as required by a stern dean of students named Cy Lambert. As I walked into the dance, a wave of noise struck me with such force that I reeled out the door—which may have been, of course, what my student hosts intended. I never went again.

Two things strike me about this generation and noise. One thing is that young people are never without sound. They live with and by it. They do not need quiet even to study. It is as if they require auditory stimulus to be certain they are alive, plugged into the world. Thus, when it happens that silence intrudes, they are uncertain that their life force is there to sustain their existence. It is not breath which sustains life but sound.

The other matter—which I first encountered at William and Mary—is the volume of noise students enjoy. A walk around the Wake Forest campus on a weekend night is deafening to older folks. It is perhaps deafening to the students as well if reported hearing losses are as we read. But there is clearly a new aesthetic at work in which the sound is so consuming that it absorbs the listeners. This music passes beyond pain and pleasure and beyond musical communication. T. S. Eliot has a phrase about "Music heard so deeply that it is not heard at all, but you are the music while the music lasts." Substitute "loudly" for "deeply" and that may be some of what is going on with this generation.

I am not criticizing this new music, just wondering at how different it is. I do often wish, however, that the musical lives of students at parties made it more possible for them to talk with each other. Talk, too, is essential, and there are many things they need to talk about, especially at parties. That parties have been rendered wordless by the supremacy of sound is a sad, and even dangerous, condition.

Given my condition, I will never be able to experience this new musical aesthetic. The pain would be real and not metaphorical. Most of all, however, I want for myself and my students that they find closets of solitude, sanctuary and, most blessed of all, silence. The voice of God is not in the storm or the whirlwind.

He speaks to us in the stillness of silence.

# Are you a Conservative or a Liberal?

 ew descriptors in our social and political vocabulary are more commonly invoked to describe persons, institutions, ideals, or ideas than "liberal" or "conservative." Which of these do you use to describe yourself? We will avoid here the artful politician's dodge, which is to deny ownership of either term. That is just a political dodge, no more. Gilbert and Sullivan, in this as in so many things, spoke the truth in one of their delightful tunes from *Iolanthe*:

> *I always think it's comical*
> *That nature always does contrive*
> *That every boy and every girl*
> *Who's born into the world alive*
> *Is either a little liberal*
> *Or else a little conservative!*

The idea that everyone is just born liberal or conservative (in the tune it rhymes with "alive") may overstate the matter, but these words are of wide and important application. I propose in this essay a one-question test, the answer to which will determine whether you should be called a "little liberal" or a "little conservative."

First, note that both words are emotionally charged, negatively and positively. To be liberal is a good thing if it means open and free-spirited but bad if it means licentious (libertine) or wasteful (as in "liberal" spending). To be conservative is bad if it means hidebound and closed minded but good if it means to exercise caution and maintain standards.

Liberal comes from the Latin for "free," and few concepts are more positively honored in a democratic society than freedom and its verbal relatives. Conservative has Latin origins meaning to "keep safe" or "preserve," and the conservation movement—from historic houses to trees and works of art—bears witness to the appeal of the word's conceptual power. (I should note that both words give rise to humorous asides. For example, the classics scholar F. M. Cornford once remarked that "nothing should be done for the first time," And Robert Frost said that a liberal is so open minded that "he wouldn't take his own side in a quarrel.")

Thus, to call yourself or someone else one of these words is fraught with feelings good or bad, which makes these terms politically useful as well as dangerous. That this language is emotive as well as descriptive makes clarity even more difficult to achieve and even more important.

Hence, in reducing this quite complex political and linguistic matter to a test with just one question, I am offering clarity in both word and fact where there is confusion and misunderstanding. Given the importance of these words, this undertaking is of similar importance.

I had an experience in the late sixties that put this question to my mind in graphic terms. I was in New York for the summer, participating as a lecturer in a program at the Lincoln Center. I lived that summer in an apartment building owned by a religious organization, which also contained dormitories occupied by student missionaries. Each morning, I would see these students leave, in pairs, dressed alike, carrying pamphlets to be distributed. In the evening, they would return. I seldom saw them otherwise, but these young people seemed, as I watched them come and go, to be constrained and limited. Something about them made me sad.

A short walk away was an entrance to Central Park, where I often went. Just inside the park was a gathering place for another group of young people, hippies or flower children, as they were called. Drugs were openly consumed, and many of those gathered there had the glazed look of intoxication. Their dress and manner were weird and bizarre to me, even though I had lived all my adult life on a university campus. It was a gathering drawn from the musical *Hair*. I would pass this group, feeling worried and distressed about them, only to return to my apartment to witness the other group returning from their missionary rounds.

The question struck me one day like a jolt: If my children were in one or the other of these groups, which would I prefer them to be? If I were to join one or the other, which company would seem least uncongenial or repugnant? Recognizing that either alternative is undesirable, which would I choose? Given the extremes, am I a liberal or a conservative? What about you? If pressed, which party would you join?

It was many years later before the one-question test to answer this question occurred to me. It is quite straightforward: Do you believe that the description of the condition of humanity presented in the Biblical story of Adam and Eve is correct? I am not discussing whether you think the story is literally true or not, but whether you agree or disagree with its lesson about human nature.

Let's briefly review what that lesson is. Adam and Eve were created perfect, but temptation (the serpent, the apple, the knowledge of good and evil) destroyed that perfection, leaving a "fallen" and essentially sinful creature. According to this view, human beings are incapable of acting rightly on a consistent basis, and human redemption requires supernatural divine grace.

The story of our inhumanity to our brothers and sisters is thus no accident or surprise. It is the story of a being whose nature is flawed and whose acts flow from that nature. It is thus never surprising or unusual to find evil or wrongdoing, even on the part of the most prominent or respectable persons: a local minister embezzles the savings of his parishioners, a woman poisons several men, a man sexually molests his friend's daughter. Does this conduct seem inhuman or all too human to you?

This account of sinful human nature has always had its

critics and dissenters. Especially since the Enlightenment, the idea of progress has exercised growing influence. Human beings, too, according to these views, have progressed. From our primitive, uncivilized state, the race has evolved to the point that our impulses are, or can be, under the control of reason and society. Given education and opportunity, men and women will act rightly, from principle, reflecting the general welfare of themselves and others.

Especially in our century, the idea that change means progress yields the belief that human beings are improving. There is a long tradition of utopian idealism, premised on the belief that, given proper social arrangements, humans are capable of an ideal social existence. (Idealism is just that. It's not perfect. Some utopian thought involves totalitarian schemes, reflecting the belief that human beings can be perfected only if personal freedom to choose is abolished. This kind of utopian thought derives from the Biblical tradition.)

Thus, when people do wrong, we need to find some explanation of evil other than human nature itself. Evil has causes other than evildoers—in childhood abuse, in poverty or lack of opportunity, or in other social explanations. The local newspaper opines that "The causes [of crime] mostly start before the future criminals are out of diapers," and castigates as "mean-spirited" a politician who says that some people are "born bums."

Conservatives believe the Adam and Eve story. The church, the state (which is the depersonalized and institutionalized use of violence), and the family must be empowered to exert force to control the unruly passions that govern the human heart.

Liberals do not believe the Biblical narrative. Evil is not in the human heart but in the corrupting environments that cause humans to act in ways they would not by nature choose to act. Liberals thus are critics generally of the political and ecclesiastical authorities because such institutions are premised on the need for repressive power to check human nature's evil impulse. Liberals call many social instruments "repressive." By that they mean repressive of human freedom and choice. Conservatives say that these powers are necessary to restrain the evil human beings would otherwise do.

In answering the following test, you are not allowed the politician's dodge. You can't say that there is a little bit of truth on both sides. The disagreement involved is fundamental and categorical, and there is no middle ground.

## The Test

Select one:

I believe that human nature is essentially good, and to eliminate evil we must remedy the social causes that are at the root of human evil.

I believe that the Biblical account is right, and human nature must be controlled by instruments of social order to permit human beings to function as society requires.

Now you know whether you are a "little liberal" or a "little conservative."

# The Sunday Self

O ne of the enduring memories of my childhood concerns how different Sunday was from the other days of the week. There were rituals of preparation—Sunday school lessons to be read, shoes to be shined, and, yes, a more thorough than usual bath and inspection. Then on Sunday there were special things to do, places to go, food to eat—all of which made this day. Part of this difference lives in our language if it has not disappeared. We speak of "Sunday" clothes, and our "Sunday" best, and "Sunday" manners, at least those of us of a certain age do.

My childhood was spent in a small Alabama town with a large extended family. Sunday meant going to my grandparents for dinner (which comes at noon, the evening meal in the South was then "supper"), usually joined by an army of relatives. But Sunday was not like other holidays when the cousins converged. There were games we could not play, and places we could not go. Perhaps my most vivid and frequent recollection is of sitting on the porch in a swing or rocking chair listening to adult talk. It was a quieter day than Christmas or the fourth of July or other holidays.

Sunday was not a regular day, and on Sunday I was not a regular person. What was I learning on those Sundays? What were the messages being felt as well as heard? One is obvious. The self we show to God (and our relatives!) is a prettified version of the regular person—dressed up and on our best behavior. The boy who goes to church and visits with the Lord hardly recognizes himself. The clothes are uncomfortable and never quite fit. The speech at church is unfamiliar (though I now believe that the removal of the King James Bible from popular use is among the most serious losses for religion, language, and education in this century). The gap between the religious self and real life was learned early.

But I have come to believe that the Sunday lesson went beyond the notion that the regular Monday-to-Saturday Tom could not talk to the Lord. There was another more pervasive life lesson. We are all aware as adults of the difference between the public self, the person we show to the world, and the private self, the self we know inwardly, the person we are. This distinction between the public and private person is one of life's most important and difficult realities. I think I started to learn this distinction on the Sundays of my childhood when I was scrubbed, dressed, and mannered for a day so that I appeared to be the ideal public boy my parents wanted me to be and wanted me to think that I should become.

The public self is always scrubbed and mannered, always in control of his emotions, doing and saying the right things.

That private self is often insecure, uncertain, and fearful—fearful above all perhaps that others will see through the public facade and find out just how unlike the public personality this other person is. The "Sunday Tom" was barely acquainted with the other lad.

There is something odd and surprising about this basic public-private division of life. We all know from our own cases the vast difference between the presented self and the private person. Yet we all tend to take the public presented selves of others at face value. We know this distinction in ourselves, but we never assume the same difference in others. We are shocked and surprised when we discover that some public person we accept at face value has a private reality that contradicts the person we think we know. Sometimes these discoveries are horrifying—we discover some terrible face behind the mask—but more often, the revelations of the private selves of others in moments of intimate disclosure build relationships and reassure us that in our private fears and insecurities we are not alone. We may respect and admire the public selves of others, even those we know at a distance like public figures, but relationships of affection and friendship attach to the private self with all its emotionality and vulnerability.

The closer our experiences bring us to the primal, elemental human emotional realities, the more we enter the domain of the inner private self. Food is basic to life. Eating disorders plague many of us. It seems so easy: why can't I just stop eating and lose weight? Because food meets inner needs unrelated to nutrition. I struggle to eat what I should and leave off what I should avoid. Our sense of emotional security or insecurity and our attachments to those we love are the primary ingredients in human happiness, yet few of us manage these vital relationships in accordance with the scripts our Sunday selves know so well. Privately we are driven by irrational emotions and passions, but the presented self never is. The sexual impulse bedevils the inner self, yet the public self is presented as all but immune to such feelings. These are the divisions of life I was learning on the Sundays of my Alabama boyhood.

I have spoken as if the private self is the "real" self, and we often think that way. The truth is more complicated. We are in reality both these selves, the combination of our "Sunday" self and the weekday person. That weekday person strives with varying success to be that Sunday self, but that rationalized and ideal person often cannot cope with those fundamental realities with which we must all contend. The core human realities—life and death, love and hate, fears, jealousies, sexual and other passions—do not follow the dictates of the Sunday self. As Pascal said, "The heart has its reasons, which reason knows nothing of."

For some reason, this lesson in elementary psychology—if it can loosely be called that—always strikes me vividly at freshman convocation. I speak to the gathered assembly of new students and parents at a tense moment. The cars have been unloaded and the program for parents is ending. Everyone is tired from the travel, the move, and the anxiety over the impending departure. Excitement is yielding to anxiety and grief. The parents are about to depart, leaving their child—a child no more—never again to be parents in the same sense.

Childhood is over. Everyone feels the anxiety of the moment—students trying to connect to new people and facing new challenges in an unfamiliar place, parents confronting a symbolic death in the family, and the college community attempting to make a good start to the academic year.

Almost everyone privately is tense. The anxiety of the moment is palpable. Yet as I stand to speak and look out across the assembly, it could be almost any regular convocation. People are calmly sitting and politely listening. They assume, I suspect, that their private turmoil is unique to themselves, masking the fears and doubts which fill the moment because of the moment it is. The public face of others is taken, as it always is, as the real face. I am struck with the urge to lead a common confessional, to let everyone cry and moan or pray, or hug each other, to let these private fears be acknowledged and the private selves comforted.

I do no such thing, of course. President Tom is the true son of Sunday Tom, and I do the presidential thing and sustain the conspiracy we are practicing together. Yet my private self feels the fear of these children at the end of childhood and the loss these parents face as they head toward a home strangely quiet, and I grieve that we ignore this moment when we need and might seek and receive consolation.

—————————————

SEPTEMBER, 1992

117

EDUCATION

# Our Public Schools

Public schools are beleaguered institutions. Report after report tell us that the schools are awash in mediocrity, likening their influence in our society to that of a foreign subversive power.

Whose schools are these anyway? We have the very institutions we create. We cannot even blame Washington since these schools are under local jurisdiction. If our schools do not measure up, accountability begins at home.

We have never given public education adequate support, we have not made teaching the equivalent of other professions of comparable importance, and we have not measured the value of teaching against its awesome responsibility, namely, the intellectual preparation of our common future. For generations we counted on a captive female professional population secured only by the absence of other options. The women's movement has opened professions to women, and education must now compete with medicine, business, and law for the best female talent. This is a benefit to women and to society at large, but it threatens public education at its source: good teachers.

Further compounding the problems of our schools, we continue to enlarge the purpose of school. Presented with fundamental societal problems our standard response is to teach it in the schools. If the country fears the communist challenge, our answer is to teach civics courses of questionable merit. Faced with the automotive revolution, our schools are now required to teach everyone to drive. When the advent of birth control pills and the sexual revolution yield a social crisis, our response is sex education in the school.

Drug education is another example, but by far the most serious instance of using the schools to resolve nonacademic social issues is that of racial integration. The question is not whether integration is legally and morally correct—it is. But why should the public schools, almost alone, be asked to bear the social responsibility of eliminating discrimination and securing racial equality?

"Integrate the schools, and the schools will integrate society" may sound like good policy, but the implementation of such policy placed an impossible burden on the public schools, making the schools targets of opposition from every side. These controversies have something to do with social justice but very little to do with teaching kids to read and write. Virtually every school system in the country has been shaken by the upheaval of integration. This was too great a task for any single institution, especially one so subject to pressure. Society may gain, but education and the schools lose.

A theme runs through these examples. Issues that properly belong to the home, church, or the courts are too easily relegated to the schools. These are complex matters that bear on every aspect of our common life—after all, something has to be done about illicit drug use and automobiles and sex education and social justice—but what? We are not quite sure. A safe and painless palliative is simply to give the problems to the schools and require a course in it.

Our public schools have become our social pantry. We dispose of unsightly problems and enjoy the fleeting sense of having done something worthwhile. This practice is bad for the schools in the achievement of their primary mission, and hence ultimately bad for society.

Meanwhile, Johnny cannot read, write, or do sums. Dare we ask why? Dare we blame his teachers? We have the schools we have made. These are our public schools.

# Should a University Be
# Run Like a Business?

Discussion of educational administration invariably turns to the question, "Why shouldn't a university be run like a business?" Here is my standard reply.

First, we must challenge the assumption that businesses are all well run and managed. "Like a business" is meant honorifically. Many businesses are poorly run and fail as a result of poor management. There is nothing about business as such that guarantees good management.

The basic reason why a university cannot be run like a business is fundamental: a university is not a business. The purpose of a university is knowledge, not profit. From that intellectual mission springs everything about the university, including its organizational theory.

The organization of the university must reflect the structure of the academy, which is not, despite appearances, a regular hierarchy. An organizational chart of a university can be drawn, but it will not actually reflect the workings of the institution. A descriptive chart would show small circles representing different constituencies within a larger circle representing the entire institution. A university is composed of groups—faculty, students, staff, alumni, trustees, educational and professional organizations, and so on. All these groups, but primarily the faculty, must be consulted in the process of policy formation. The traditional organizational chart with a CEO (a terrible expression in view of these ideas) that makes decisions for subordinates misrepresents the way universities function.

The traditions of what is called "collegial governance" or "shared governance" are strong in the academy, as they should. Collective bargaining in universities was stalled by a ruling of the Supreme Court that decided that faculty was functionally managerial. The university is about education, and the faculty and students do the definitive work of the institution—yet many other university groups are also part of this corpus. They too must be consulted and heard. This can be, and sometimes is, a chaotic environment.

The university president's task is to see that the separate and numerous constituencies of the university are consulted appropriately and that policies that reflect the common, not the separate, interests of the university are developed. The president is responsible for the large, enclosing circle. Each university constituency has a separate set of concerns. These will partly coincide and partly conflict with the interests of other groups. The president, along with the trustees, are the guardians of the interests of the entire university, not of its separate parts.

The president must articulate common institutional interests and explain and promote them to various groups. There are inevitable limitations on this process. People have closest loyalties to the smallest groups to which they belong and so will have a clear understanding, therefore, of the needs of their own groups and less sympathy for the interests of others. This results in competition and conflict among these groups, which can be intense. The president and the administration, as arbiters of competing claims for and with the trustees, must choose among these interests. This environment accounts in part for the fact that administrators are seldom universally loved by all groups. There are too many interests, too few resources. Administrators say no more often than yes. Turnover among presidents, vice presidents, and deans is high.

University leaders are usually products of the faculty system. In an ironic twist on an old adage in the university, "Those who can, teach; those who can't go into administration." A colleague once commented, "Half my faculty thinks they could do my job as well as I do. Half thinks anyone could do as well." Leadership in a university is a complex enterprise. Universities attract, in the first instance, people interested in ideas, not in management. Of those who might be administrative leaders, just a few find the right opportunity to develop their skills. There are a few programs to give faculty members, while still early in their careers, the opportunity to consider administration and to prepare themselves for leadership opportunities.

The university, so able to provide leaders for the rest of society, needs urgently to turn its own resources to its own leadership needs. Universities are wonderful places. Faculty are interesting people, the best minds we have. Students are at the most formative point in their lives. It's easy to respect and have affection for these people and the important work they do together, and that work brings joy to those of us privileged to work and serve among them.

# *Language Lessons*

It is hard to believe that in 1937 Rhett Butler's on-screen "damn" could have created a public sensation. Canons regarding obscenity in language have gone a long way the wrong way in half a century. While I try to be accepting of inevitable changes in social mores, I have little tolerance regarding foul language. I advocate a return to the fabled practice of washing offending mouths out with soap. Let me offer, therefore, what I concede to be a futile protest against the ordinary use of four-letter words.

Our American English language lacks rich resources for swearing. I am told that other languages are infinitely better suited for the purpose of speaking, as sometimes is necessary, all of one's mind, even the vilest parts. Our language offers to the would-be swearer just a few theological and bodily expressions. These meager resources we have depleted by common use.

Since our few expressions are used over coffee to discuss the flower show, we are without any resources with which to tell somebody off emphatically. Our linguistic shells spent, we fire verbal blanks. Our cursing arsenal has been raided and made ordinary. By popular use, swearing loses expressive and emotive power. Our most emphatic language has been trivialized and rendered impotent. In this not-so-important respect, our language has been deprived of a function.

The loss of the obscene diminishes language in other ways. As the obscene becomes commonplace, our respect and regard for the language falls. Language is a strange and remarkable achievement. It is, or is at least correlative of, thought itself. What we think, we say. What we say is what we do. Language that has lost its sense of obscene fails to incorporate in speech a sense of the prohibited, the disallowed. That absence will surely be reflected in thought and subsequently in deed.

A proper respect for language begins with respect for its rules, namely, grammar. It is not enough to understand words. Language is an instrument of communication, but it is not merely that. Language is the chief vehicle for our whole relationship to the world and others. First and foremost, I urge a return to the requirement that schools require people to memorize masterpieces of the language, especially our greatest poetry and the central passages of the King James Bible. Familiarity and repetition create appreciation of the beauty and communicative power in language well-used. As close as I come to believing in magic and its incantations is my faith in the transforming power of expressive language.

Second, we should require periodic breaks from the mass media. Days or weeks without TV or radio and their linguistic excesses would do much to restore balance to our language. In these breaks, parents could talk to children, friends might visit each other, and young people should meet at their places of gathering (without deafening music) and actually get acquainted. "Visiting" is a dying practice that needs a revival.

If there were more of this talk—human conversation—and less of the passively received excesses of the media, a sense of the proper and improper speaking might be generated. In that case, when it becomes necessary to "cuss out," someone, we would have to use words to do the job. Language might be seen as an instrument of beauty as well as truth.

# Academics and Eggheads

There is a story—doubtless apocryphal—of a college that had a lovely gate at its entrance bearing its name. On the reverse side, visible upon exit, the students had created an equally elegant script that read, "The Real World." That sign, if it existed, was a clever statement of a pervasive and powerful point of view that the academy is other-worldly, that the concerns of the university are not those of the "real" world. Academics and eggheads, this view holds, are out of touch with the things that matter in the flux of real life, hence thus the negative implications of these expressions.

This notion of the unreality and unrelatedness of the concerns of the academy may be, and often is, a statement of lighthearted anti-intellectualism. Professors are slightly comic figures, absent-minded, and interested in issues of no practical relevance, so many versions of the "how many angels can dance on the head of a pin" question. I want to reject this characterization of academics and eggheads as erroneous, even dangerous. These views of the academy misunderstand dangerously the forces at work in the real world.

A friend recently told me about a new course he was teaching with the title "The Makers of the Twentieth Century." I asked for the list of century makers: Darwin, Marx, Freud, Einstein. Darwin changed our understanding of our relationship to nature. Marx was a social theorist. Freud forced a new comprehension of the forces at work in human nature and society. Einstein revolutionized the physical theories that had been dominant for three hundred years and created modern physics with all its promise and peril.

All were thinkers, eggheads. They were men of ideas. The lesson here is simple but profound: to change the world most fundamentally is to change the way people think. Ideas are more powerful than kings and princes. The work and concern of the university is with ideas, and it is a profound error to regard academic concerns as merely academic (to make my point with the word). Ideas and those who create and transmit them rule the world.

According to commonly held views of eggheads and academics, the things that matter in the real world are instruments of power of various kinds—political, economic, or military. Exponents of this viewpoint might concede the influence of Marx, whose ideas had powerful political outcomes, and Einstein, whose ideas, to be simpleminded, made bombs. But that concession is just my point. What these men did was to conceive revolutions of the mind. Other lesser figures take these ideas into the world where they change history. The ideas come first. Philosophers, theoreticians, thinkers, and eggheads are kings in the domain of the mind.

But the power of Darwin is, if anything, greater than Marx or Einstein. His suggestion of the "survival of the fittest" came to be regarded as a social and economic as well as biological idea. The evolutionary metaphor runs through much social and economic thought. The struggle against Darwin goes on as reported in your newspaper because he proclaimed a new conception of the relationship of human nature to nature. At stake is nothing less than the human place in the universe, our relationship to the rest of the natural order.

Ideas about the nature of the human person are the most important ideas because of their universal applicability. From self-understanding emerges all else that humans are prepared to believe and what they are prepared to do in support of those beliefs. Sigmund Freud was both creator and expositor of one of this century's most prevalent beliefs—the hidden truth behind the facade of convention and artifice, the hidden reality that governs and controls belief and behavior. That idea has given impulse to almost all twentieth century art. The ideas of Freud about the role of unconscious beliefs and the role of sexuality in human life, once thought radical, are now accepted as commonplace.

The princes of kingdoms and the generals of great armies wield great power, but that power is ever and always limited by the beliefs of subjects and soldiers. Revolutions begin in the mind. Values, beliefs, hopes, and aspirations form the context within which power of any sort over people and society can be exercised. The minds that create this context of social belief are the ultimate rulers in the domain of the intellect. Giants of commerce, government, and the military are vassals to those who are kings of the intellect.

The university is the place in society where these ruling ideas are formulated, tested, and debated. This responsibility is inevitably disturbing to structures of belief, which are the creations of sets of ideas held sacred by existing institutions and orthodoxies. This ultimate duty of the university to the life of the mind requires careful and thoughtful exercise because the social outcomes of these ideas in the world are revolutionary. Existing ideologies attempt to enshrine their own orthodoxies and fix belief in final formulations. But this process of the creation, refinement, and transmission of ideas must be fostered and nurtured as only the human response to our finite grasp of an infinite universe.

Aristotle opens his *Metaphysics* with the statement that humans by nature desire to know. That impulse to know is the center of the university's own commitment to unfettered thought and the social responsibility the university bears in the present and for the future.

Academics and eggheads? They are our mentors, guides, and rulers into the realm of belief. In the real world, we are but slaves to beliefs of which they are lords.

# Fund-Raising

A frequent remark made to me about my position is "Isn't it terrible to be always raising money?" There is a common perception that presidents spend their energies raising money and that it is a very distasteful business. Derrick Bok has been quoted as saying, "Presidents are beggars who live in big houses."

I would like to challenge this perspective about fund-raising. It is, in my experience, wholly mistaken. Wake Forest University is entering a major capital campaign and I am now spending considerable amounts of time on this effort. However, fund-raising as such has not dominated my calendar over my years in office. Moreover, nothing about development work resembles begging, nor does it have any resemblance to coercion. Fund-raising contacts are a positive part of my life as president. Let me tell you why.

Fund-raising is simply part of institutional advocacy,

something I do all the time. As president, I am my institution's chief spokesman and advocate. Some of that advocacy takes the form of fund-raising. Much of it does not. But presenting the strengths and opportunities of Wake Forest is a primary task of this office, one which I am proud and honored to perform. Fund-raising arises from the great tradition of voluntary charitable giving in this country. It is one of our nation's most notable and noble features. Successful individuals and companies have a shared commitment to the creation of strong educational and human service institutions. No other society shares this commitment to voluntarism and philanthropy on the American model. That cultural commitment is the social background from which development work arises. Many Americans who are successful want that success to account for public as well as private benefit. Were individuals or corporations not possessed of a charitable intent, no president would ever be talking to them about a university's needs and opportunities. This activity is part of a great tradition.

The university in America is, for the best of reasons, a favored object of charitable giving. The university engages in two of society's most basic undertakings: the pursuit of truth as the basis of civilized life and the preparation of the young for lives of constructive service. Education is the construction of the future. Philanthropy, among other things, aims to shape the future. Many donors return to their schools something for the values received in their own lives. Universities offer ways whereby the values and interests of contributors can be given permanent influence within the structure of the university. A scholarship or a professorship is a permanent contribution to the institution and to many individuals over many years.

There are often established relationships between donors and educational institutions. These relationships mean that the donor has a thorough understanding of the institution and its needs. The presentation of those needs by the president or others is a continuation of an important relationship. Development thus has nothing to do with coercion. It has everything to do with the interests and needs of the university in relationship to the values and interests of donors.

Such relationships bring deep personal satisfaction to the donor as well as value to the institution. The Carswell family of Charlotte created a scholarship program at Wake Forest many years ago. Until her death, Mrs. Carswell came each year for a birthday party given for her at Wake Forest by the Carswell Scholars. She presented plaques to the graduating seniors, commemorating their graduation as Carswell Scholars, and one of the scholars would express appreciation for the group to Mrs. Carswell. I sat with her on several of these occasions. Nothing in her life, she told me, gave her more personal satisfaction than the knowledge that her late husband's generosity had contributed to the education of so many fine young people.

I learned the meaning of giving to the giver in my first experience with a major donor. I was a new administrator with no experience at all in development. My institution had a desperate need for space for teaching the fine arts. As our plans progressed, a donor appeared who wanted to build this space. He was a successful man who had no formal education beyond high school. He had, however, acquired a deep appreciation for the arts as an adult. His life had been immensely enriched by these interests, and he regretted that he had not been exposed to these activities earlier. This building had a deep, personal significance for him. It pleased him that young people were being given opportunities he had been denied. I remember walking through the building with him after it had been dedicated and was in active use. Painters, musicians, dancers, and others were at work in every room. At the end of the tour, I thanked him again for his generosity. "No, I should thank you," he said. "Nothing I have ever done has given me so much satisfaction." We remained friends until his death. It was a warm and satisfying relationship for both of us, grounded in his generosity and his pleasure at the meaning of his success for generations of students and faculty.

There are many such stories. Successful people want their success to serve the values they cherish. Their values find expression in contributions to the university whose programs can make future opportunities for many.

As we enter this Heritage and Promise Campaign, Wake Forest has a wonderful story to tell and wonderful people to tell it and to whom it will be told. Wake Forest has a clear and compelling vision of its future promise and a large and growing donor public to support our aspirations. To participate in this campaign is for me a source of genuine satisfaction. I hope you will find it so.

---

THIS ARTICLE APPEARED IN THE MAY 1999 ISSUE OF
THE PHILANTHROPY JOURNAL OF NORTH CAROLINA.

# LEADERSHIP

# Leadership and Teaching in the American University

I n what follows, I will reflect on the culture and organization of the university as a distinct institutional type. I suggest that the university climate militates against the exercise of leadership conceived of as traditional executive authority. This presents a growing problem in a period in which external regulation and demands for accountability are requiring the university to behave more like a traditional corporate entity, thus requiring effective and efficient leadership. Legislators, trustees, and stakeholders impose these demands. This central dilemma for the university leader has its own equally distinct solution. I will try to suggest a way, drawn from teaching, that the task of university leadership can be exercised effectively while reflecting the particular organizational character of the university.

In leadership studies, it is common to distinguish between "leadership" and "management." Leadership is required for institutional change—the preservation or alteration of mission and the maintenance of strategic vision. Management addresses the tasks of regular "maintenance and repair." While my uses of these terms in this essay will reflect ordinary use that may blur these distinctions, it is leadership, not management, that the university generally resists (though some leaders have managerial wounds as well!).

In the university setting, "administration" refers to a group of people as well as a set of tasks. The term "administration" can, of course, range over leaders and managers, leadership and management. My concern is directed to the role of leadership in the university.

Another explanatory note: I set out these ideas to present them—I had no idea where or when—for a nonuniversity audience. This conference changed the audience but not the entire scheme of the essay. Some of these observations may be self-evident to academic audiences, but they are worth reviewing.

## The Essential Nature of Leadership

From long observation and experience in groups of every sort and size, I am convinced that leadership is essential to the success of all forms of collective enterprise. Understood generally as the process by which people unite to achieve common or shared purposes and projects, leadership is a sine qua non of successful collective endeavor. Groups may have good ideas, ample resources, and promising opportunities, but failure threatens unless and until the essential human resources are mobilized by effective leadership.

I came to the subject of leadership years back as the result of a dramatic experience—a literal epiphany. I was a relatively new academic vice president at the University of Alabama at Birmingham. The legislature in Alabama would regularly appropriate funds based on estimated tax income that predictably exceeded actual funds receipted. The politics of this deplorable fiscal practice made it too tempting to avoid. "Proration" was the practice of reducing state budgets during the fiscal year to the level of actual income. During the year in question, proration had been severe and academic budgets had been cut several times. Another round of proration promised to be an administrative ordeal of the first order. The easy reductions already had been taken.

Proration could not be uniformly applied to all schools and departments. Some areas were experiencing enrollment growth and others were in decline. New and strategically important programs required sustained budgetary support. After meeting with the deans, individually and in groups, I gave each dean a target for expense reduction in the various school budgets. As you can imagine, this was a process fraught with conflict and controversy. Trips to professional meetings to present research results were being cancelled. Equipment necessary to scholarly inquiry was not to be purchased. Classes were to be made bigger or teaching loads increased. Each dean knew lots of areas, not in their own schools of course, where these reductions could and should be taken. In this process, a miserable time was had by all!

Late in the afternoon on the day the budget reduction reports were due, my feet were propped up on the desk as I watched the sunset out the window, pondering my woes. My assistant came with the reports, which he had separated into two groups. One group, he said, had done what was necessary, but the other group "would need more work"—that is, had not met their budgeted reductions. Delay, defer, and deny is often a bureaucratic strategy of choice, and most of the deans had far more practice than I. Setting these reports in front of me on the desk, my assistant said good night and left.

My feet remained on the desk as I looked at the two stacks of reports before me, dreading the assignment ahead. No one relishes conflict over money. There was thus more pain to mete out, more arm wrestling with deans seeking to protect their cherished programs and their status as defenders of their faculties.

As I reflected on the matters at hand, a thought suddenly struck with the force of revelation. Without looking, I knew which reports were in what stacks—and I knew with certainty. The reason struck with a similar force. Among the group of deans reporting to me, I had good leaders and I had poor leaders. The good leaders had met the requirement, and the poor leaders had not. Leadership sorted the reports. In this moment of insight, the next thought, which also jolted me, was that no one had mentioned the word "leadership" to me since I was a Boy Scout many years—lifetimes—ago. It was a moment of illumination and clarity that brought utter certainty and conviction.

I knew from that moment that I would be different, and

that my conception of my responsibilities would change. My job—contrary to what I thought—was not in those reports. My task was the people whose job it was to prepare the reports. My job was not the budget. My challenge was to develop the capacity of those who were responsible for the budget. Despite the fact that I occupied a senior executive position, no one had explained this distinction to me. Leadership was the missing ingredient.

This moment of epiphany was so vivid that I still recall the details of it with clarity. As it felt at the time, it was a moment of transition. As an academic, I, of course, headed to the library and in time discovered James MacGregor Burns' classic work, *Leadership*, a book that became for me, and remains, an essential guide.

Burns' work had a substantial scholarly influence, establishing the subject of leadership as a topic of more than historic interest. When Burns came to Wake Forest University in the mid-1980s to lecture, I had a lengthy and unforgettable visit with him. Among other things, he told me that when researching this work in the New York City Public Library he found no card catalog entry for "leadership." There were listings under "leaders," but the generic subject "leadership" had yet to be recognized as a separate domain of study.

I have continued to engage the subject of leadership, which has brought me further blessings and benefits. When I came to Wake Forest, I learned of the Center for Creative Leadership (CCL) in Greensboro. William Friday, then head of the University of North Carolina and Chairman of CCL's board, invited me to serve. I have done so ever since, and in time I succeeded Bill

Friday as Chair of the Board of Governors. My opportunity to be a part of an institution where some of the world's most important leadership research and training is conducted has been a constant source of interest and, indeed, inspiration. Wake Forest is pleased to cohost this session with CCL as an extension of CCL's work into the special domain of university leadership.

## Context Matters

One key axiom of CCL's research is that leadership is not a generic set of influences to be exercised in the same way in any and every institutional setting. While all organizations have leadership requirements, how those requirements are exercised will differ radically in military, business, charitable, or volunteer institutions. Leadership must reflect the nature and purpose of the institution and be exercised in conformity with the mission and structure being served. There is no such thing as leadership generically effective in every situation. There is only leadership in a specific institutional context.

The American university is a highly specialized, even unique, institution of great and growing importance to our nation and to the world. In the information economy, the university produces the essential economic resource: the trained intelligence of our people. The research mission of the university, in science and in culture, is a constant source of intellectual experimentation, novelty, and innovation.

The university preserves and interprets the best of what human intelligence has created and written. It retains our cultural and intellectual memory and thus the identity not only of the American nation but also of many nations. As such, universities preserve and interpret the records of the past while creating the ideas and leaders for the future. The university is a repository of past achievement and the foundation of future innovation.

In America, the university is a uniquely democratic institution where ideas and ideals compete in the free-for-all of the intellectual marketplace. The public often regards this marketplace with dismay, believing that some of the ideas proffered are outrageous or dangerous. Indeed, they sometimes are. But we are all beneficiaries of the maintenance of this intellectual free-for-all, which ensures that no orthodoxy is free from evaluation and criticism. This ferment is essential to the genius of the university and to the democratic genius that is America. The American university is created by and in turn sustains democratic institutions.

It follows, of course, that the leadership needs and challenges of the university must reflect this remarkable and challenging institutional environment. It is an organization whose very culture is resistant to the exercise of leadership. Such resistance is a consequence of the intellectual ferment by which the institution lives.

In addition, this resistance derives from the highly decentralized systems by which universities are organized and governed. Schools, departments, institutes, centers, and the like form a network of associations that are variously organized, funded, and governed. Despite what an organizational chart might look like, no ordinary organizational structure exists to govern by means of a traditional hierarchy. Inevitably, commitment and identity in the university tend to be directed to the parts rather than the whole. I am reminded of one of Clark Kerr's most memorable aphorisms: "A university is a group of mutually antagonistic fiefdoms held together by a parking problem!"

At the same time, however, the external demand for and requirement of leadership and accountability in the university is growing from public and private agencies. We thus face a growing dilemma. As an organization resistant to the exercise of central authority, we nonetheless confront public requirements for accountability (increasingly so) that demand leadership authority. Indeed, one consequence of the university having moved to the center of the economic order is that oversight and the expectation of effective outcomes have inevitably followed. With growing influence has come growing oversight.

The consumer movement has overtaken American higher education in recent decades. A symptom of the rise of consumerism, as well as a cause of it, is the proliferation of college guides and rankings. These are the "consumer reports" for our "industry," and shoppers compare price, value, and durability as they might when choosing a car or a dishwasher. Consumers demand value and measures of accountability, and consumers serve in the legislature and on university boards.

As the university has gained importance and influence, it has attracted the attention of government regulators of every sort: local, state, and federal. The days when our schools were "society's pets"—places for the youthful gaiety of football games, parties, and fun—are long past. We must meet and pass every standard, legal and regulatory, that other large institutions, public and private, confront. Whether it is the IRS, the FTC, the EPA, HIPPA, OSHA, or any of the other regulatory acronyms, the university must have its regulatory house in order.

Casual, decentralized leadership systems staffed by volunteer committees are inadequate to the challenge this new regulatory environment presents. The university has been required to professionalize its administrative staff to meet these requirements, which has met with criticism on many campuses. The fact remains that regulation from external agencies must be matched and managed by competent professionals. Universities are now sometimes described by faculty, not in praise, as "bureaucratic" or "corporate." So we have become.

It is increasingly common for presidents and chancellors to be called CEO, an expression never heard a few years ago. "CEO" perhaps embodies this tension I am describing, for this very title suggests a kind and scale of authority that is uncongenial within the culture of the university.

## Organizational Nature of Universities

Given that leadership must inevitably be exercised in a particular institutional context, it is essential to appreciate the unique purposes specific to each setting. The special context of the university as an institution bears this point out.

First of all, universities themselves are remarkably different. While they may all formally do the same or similar things, their missions and cultures are different. I do not mean merely that schools differ according to type—a liberal arts college is different from a technical or community college, or a private university is different from a land grant institution. I mean rather that institutions of the same type—be they colleges or public or private universities—have quite different notions of the way in which the work of the institution is to be conducted. Universities form unique cultural environments. One fallacy of college rankings is the assumption that because universities all grant degrees, they are alike in what they do and can be compared as differing instances of the same enterprise. While similar in what they do, colleges and universities are substantially different in how they regard their purposes. Knowledge is infinite, but education is finite. Therefore, schools are inevitably specialized.

Thus, the first and most obvious task for any institutional leader is to know his or her own institution intimately and thoroughly. The need to know an institution and its people well poses a particular difficulty for a newly chosen leader, especially one coming from outside that university. In its simplest terms, the dilemma for the new leader is that the first thing a university community wants to know is what this person proposes to do. Without knowing the institution thoroughly, however, it is impossible, even dangerous, to render specific decisions except in the case of some immediate problem or crisis.

The essential strategy for the newcomer is to conduct a careful institutional audit, listening rather than speaking, and to postpone any substantive decisions until such time as the institution, its problems, and its people, are thoroughly consulted and understood. In this instance, the new leader is the pupil and the university is the teacher, helping the leader come to understand the culture and the people of this place and the challenges being faced.

What most characterizes the university as an organizational type is its radical decentralization. Sometimes centralization/decentralization is discussed as a matter of optional organizational style, some managers preferring greater or lesser autonomy in sub-units. I mean something stronger. A university by its nature and purpose must be a decentralized organization and must be administered as such. Crucially, the work of the faculty, which is the work of the university, is organized through departments, schools, and centers. That work, conducted in these organizations, is the structure upon which the entire work of the university rests.

The academic expertise gathered at the departmental level is of the highest order. That expertise, together with the traditional entitlements of academic freedom, means that academic organizations must be given broad latitude in determining what they do and how they do it. Curriculum, faculty selection and development, and student advising are of necessity under departmental authority. There can often be planning that attempts to coordinate and strengthen the work of various academic centers. But what has been called the "tyranny of departments" is a way of life and an essential feature of the university at work. The expertise determining the work of teaching and scholarship can be coordinated, but it cannot be managed without reference to its own specialized academic function.

Nor is it just the faculty and the academic organization that is the source of the decentralized influences in the university. A university is a complex set of overlapping constituencies, all of which are complexly organized, and all of which have legitimate roles to play, depending on the issues involved, in the life and work of the university. In addition to the faculty, there are students, staff, alumni, parents, the donor publics, athletic associations, legislatures, trustees, educational organizations and associations, accrediting bodies, and civic partners. This list is by no means exhaustive. Each of these groups exercises a centrifugal force, distributing the sources of influence and rendering the exercise of hierarchical executive authority impossible over a broad range of subjects. This decentralized character of the university has accelerated in recent decades by professionalization of the faculty. A generation ago, it was common for aspiring scholars following graduate school to serve a single institution for an entire career. There was such a figure in our own family, a person who occupied heroic status in our family. My grandmother's cousin, Gleason Bean, had earned a PhD—at Harvard no less. To our family in a small Alabama town, that was a singular achievement. Following graduate school, Professor Bean joined the faculty at Washington and Lee and became an essential part of the life and work of that school for his entire career. He was—I knew him in his retirement years—wedded to that school and its people. His first and only loyalty was to Washington and Lee.

Faculty members now regard their primary professional peers as colleagues in the same fields in other universities as well as their own departments. Academic careers are more likely to be mobile, and institutional loyalty has been compromised by this change in the structure and organization of American intellectual life. Faculty do not simply serve a university but a scholarly discipline. The university is a location for the practice of a profession defined by colleagues and professional organizations across the country and increasingly around the world.

As well, the Cultural Revolution of the sixties and seventies had a greater impact on the university than on most other institutions in society. Many themes of the Cultural Revolution emerged on America's campuses. An anti-institutional and anti-authoritarian attitude ("Never trust anyone over thirty!") was an essential part of that climate and culture. Of course, the graduates of that era now serve in positions of academic importance across America. This general distrust of authority further conditions the way in which leadership is regarded, especially as the external requirements of accountability are being ever more exercised toward the academy.

The substantive work of the academic environment, as well as this highly decentralized organizational setting, contributes to the atmosphere of criticism and dissent in the university. Faculty members spend their lives working to expose existing intellectual problems to critical scrutiny with the hope that new and more adequate answers to questions in their disciplines can be found. The quest for the new, the novel, the unrecognized, or even the revolutionary is the work of teaching and scholarship. No one ever won a Nobel Prize, not even a summer research grant, by claiming that the status quo is right and adequate. The academic mind lives to question existing orthodoxy and that habit of mind is prone to extend to the administrative environment of the university. There is thus an academic basis for the general concern with which faculty regard the organization and administration of the university. In the university, the old slogan is reversed: "Those who can teach, do. Those who cannot, go into administration."

Even though in various university departments the skills and work of administration, leadership, and organizational development are taught, there is general disregard for the special and specific exercise of those very same skills in the university setting. The central administration of the university represents a constant imposition of central authority that the academic community is constitutionally disposed to resist.

University leadership thus is caught between a climate and culture that resists the imposition of external standards and the demands from various public agencies that these standards be applied and applied rigorously. Perhaps in some past era, universities were generally left alone to do "their own thing" based upon a public consensus that universities were good places doing good things. The combined influence of tax revolts, consumerism, and the strength of regulatory agencies means that such a happy time is gone for good. When tax revenues decline, higher education is often high on the list of things to cut.

The university and those who exercise leadership there must find new ways to address this environment of accountability, all while preserving the special genius of the university as a place devoted to the process of discovery and to the preparation of our citizens for lives of service and accomplishment.

## Contextual Limits to Leadership in Universities

Other obstacles to leadership bear mentioning, other institutional characteristics that have the effect of limiting the leadership function in the context of the university. First, the character of the academic mind and preparation for service in the academy obviously determines the likely pool of leadership talent. To pursue a terminal degree is a formidable challenge in time, effort, and money. Such an undertaking will often require five years or more with all the attendant sacrifices of foregone income and extended student status. Those who choose this project are a special breed. They are, first and foremost, intellectually gifted, the best and brightest products of our undergraduate programs. Their talent and academic motivation have generally attracted the attention of faculty mentors, and they have received consistent academic encouragement and support. Such people have a clear academic motivation and are drawn to the domain of ideas and discovery. Those of academic inclination, when they discover that they can be paid to read, study, and write about their interests, want no other life. and can imagine no other vocation so ideal and rewarding. The last thing such people as a group have in mind for their lives is to "push paper." There is a general disdain or disregard for the work of administration—given the primacy of the academic ambitions for which they were prepared. Thus, the pool of individuals likely to be interested in and talented at administrative leadership is inevitably small, and the motivation in the academic environment for administrative work is often absent, especially in the earliest years of an academic career.

Various programs at universities and at the American Council on Education address the problem of university leadership. But the absence of a sizeable pool of academically trained and successful scholars who are interested in careers in educational leadership is a chronic problem for leadership in the academy.

Unlike in the business world, where talented young executives are put on a fast track, the academic organization generally operates according to a fixed seniority system. The position of department chair, for instance, tends to rotate among the senior staff in an academic department. This system militates against the possibility that a reasonably young academic, early in his or her career, might occupy a department chairmanship. Thus, very few young scholars are given the opportunity for the position of departmental chair to be an early formative experience for a career in educational administration.

The department chair is a critical position. Indeed, one could argue that it is the single most important administrative position in the university. In departments, members of the faculty are hired, curricula established, students advised, and, critically, promotion and tenure decided. While these decisions are reviewed outside departments, the departmental outcome is presumptively determinative. Thus, this position of chair is especially critical in understanding the work of the university at its basic level, and it provides a vitally important learning experience for potential academic leaders.

In addition, the decision of the university community in recent decades to make department chairs a rotating position has been a mixed blessing. In an earlier day when department chairs were appointed for indefinite terms, they exercised a great deal of authority, and that authority was immediately adjacent to the work of the faculty. Now that the position rotates, faculty members are often reluctant to make difficult decisions that might adversely affect their colleagues, knowing that one or the other of those colleagues will be the occupant of the chair in just a year or two.

The selection process for leadership positions in the academy, based primarily on committees representing the decentralized centers of influence in the academy, also has a limiting potential on leadership in the university. Each committee member acts to protect and support the special interests and concerns of the separate represented domains. Successful candidates must, therefore, impress the committee that nothing adverse will happen to the interests of any of the assorted programs represented by the committee.

Search committees take on a kind of corporate personality, each member typically posing the same set of questions to each candidate arising from that committee member's domain of concern. These committees also work to limit the internal contention that might result from the conflicts among and between their various interests. This effort at consensus effectively means that any committee member who objects vigorously to the candidacy of any particular individual can effectively veto that candidate. Search committees generally operate with a de facto blackball system.

Candidates with forceful and passionately held views on relevant subjects, assuming the interview process surfaces those opinions, are not likely to survive committee selection. Nor do candidates survive who are idiosyncratic or eccentric in any respect. All of us have known talented candidates whose personality cannot be chosen in a process of selection where committees are the primary vehicle.

This search process frequently works to the disadvantage

of internal candidates who have been involved in local decision making, inevitably controversial, and are regarded as problematic by disadvantaged interests. This is not always the case, of course. Knowing the personalities on the committee, internal candidates can sometimes navigate these conflicts with better information and diplomatic skills.

Fixed academic attitudes are also at work in university executive searches. A typical faculty opinion is that there is no specific and unique talent or requirement for the work of educational administration. Thus, excessive attention is given to the academic qualifications of candidates, and not enough, if any, given to the talents and competencies of effective leadership. A frustrated trustee serving on such a committee once remarked to me, "The committee acts as if they are hiring a faculty colleague or a research professor, not a leader." That frustration is often legitimate. Faculty committee members are looking naturally for people like themselves, not necessarily those with the talent of leaders.

The selection process can resemble a human demolition derby, a car race in which jalopies crash into each other until only one remaining car is moving. That car, of course, is also damaged, but it is at least running. The search process often amounts to such a process of candidate demolition and sacrifices the characteristics of a meritocratic process. It is, however, a process that often serves to protect and secure the decentralized academic interests of the committee members.

The transition period into a new position of responsibility within the university is fraught with leadership risks. The question to which everyone wants an answer is, "What is this new leader going to do?" People reasonably expect the new officer to have something substantive to say. The dilemma, of course, especially for a new person coming from the outside, is that he or she does not know what is required. Thus, new university officers go through an exceedingly difficult and challenging process of trying to establish credibility while taking a period of time—as long as possible or necessary—to ascertain what steps would be most constructive.

The old adage about having a single chance to make a first impression bears particular attention during periods of transition. A new officer must solicit advice and assistance from as many seasoned veterans as possible. Early presentations to important constituencies must be carefully crafted, with special attention to the interests and concerns of the audience. As soon as I was named president of Wake Forest University, I began to get, as you can imagine, large amounts of mail and publications from all segments of the university. I noticed immediately that no two pieces of correspondence and no two publications looked alike. There was no standard institutional signature, no standard graphic identity.

This struck me at once as a problem needing a quick solution. So, shortly after I arrived, with the help of design consultants and with the involvement of a fairly small (clearly too small) group of participants, the new administration promulgated a new logo and graphic design requirements. The result was what I did not know then to expect but should have. The new design requirements were interpreted as everything from an invasion of territorial prerogatives to an attempt to abolish the historic seal and eliminate the motto of the university. We held firm, and the new design standards were, in time, accepted. For a period, I was dubbed the "logo cop" since people would get from me copies of documents and publications marked and noted that had not meet the new design criteria.

A much broader and better process was needed. I made a mistake of some importance in a period of transition. People care, rightly so, about their own graphic identity, and control over such matters as publications is often a matter of contention. I learned from the experience.

Lastly, tenure in the executive offices of universities tends to be relatively brief. These numbers fluctuate over time. In good economic times tenures are longer. To make fundamental changes in educational programs or organizations is not of weeks or months, but of years and may often take longer than an administrator has years in office. To conceive plans, to win support for those plans, to garner the resources such plans might require, and then to put those plans in place, requires a time cycle likely to meet or exceed the expected terms of senior officials.

These frequent transitions in office are themselves an adverse factor on the leadership structure of universities. Leadership changes are disruptive, and shorter terms in office will inevitably mean reduced influence and authority in such offices.

## The Three Subjects of Leadership

Three general separate but related subjects fall under the broad interdisciplinary subject of leadership. The first involves personality: what are leaders like? This question has its origins in the charismatic or "great man" view of leadership that regards leadership as a particular form of human genius, akin to musical or artistic genius. Though more or less discredited, there still is necessary interest in the personal qualities and characteristics of those who are successful leaders.

The second general topic is the function of leadership: What is it that leaders do? This involves a general analysis of the leadership role in organizations. The functions identified range broadly from generic values and mission to strategy and planning. What leaders do is a distinct question from what leaders are like.

A third more general subject involves performance: How does leadership render organizations effective? What are the requirements, including leadership and organizational relationships, that cause groups and organizations to be maximally effective or "high performing?" Leadership is one feature, among others, of organizations that achieve their goals. I will focus on just the first of these questions: the qualities of persons required to lead effectively in the setting of the university.

There is, indeed, a social paradox when we consider the matter of leadership in America. American universities produce the finest graduates in the world. And while universities may conspire against the active creation of leadership within its ranks, other organizations and institutions do not. Indeed, business and military organizations, for example, are specifically and continually focused on leadership and leadership development. Organizations like CCL assist groups of every size and description in putting in place systems that will facilitate the development of the leadership capacity for the future. There is a great deal of public initiative and effort on this subject with the best-trained talent pool in the world.

Yet, when it comes time to fill a critical position in a place of great leadership importance, there are never enough talented applicants. In the key positions within the hierarchy of American organizational life, executives seldom report that there were ample highly qualified candidates from which to choose. All of us who do executive selection—in the university or in our other associations—can testify to this talent deficit.

Of course, many candidates are functionally qualified, having the background and experience that the position would seem to require. What is often missing, however, are those personal qualities that are always more critical than qualifications. Thus, the question of the personal as well as the functional talent of potential leaders remains central.

I wish to pose the idea that pedagogy is the process that most helpfully guides the conduct of leadership in the university. Given the university setting as it has been described, the work of leadership is best regarded as a kind of teaching, with policies and proposals being regarded as pedagogical exercises calculated to inform, explain and, in the best cases, persuade.

Teaching is a collective process involving and requiring leadership. A teacher in a classroom occupies a leadership position. At one level a deliberative rather than a practical process aimed at outcomes, teaching involves the presentation of problems for common and collective consideration, the discussion of proposed solutions to those problems, and often the selection of the solution that seems optimal after evaluation.

Teaching also presupposes a structure of authority, the definition and control of the pedagogical process being under the leadership and guidance of the teacher. However, the authority of the teacher rests in the deliberative process itself, in the mastery of the content being considered. The process of teaching generates outcomes, as all of us who have been given grades are acutely aware, so the process involves purposeful choices.

What set of personal qualities should we seek in leaders appropriate to the climate and culture of the university? The first personal requirement for leadership as a form of teaching is a passion for ideas, a love of learning. A university leader must, above all, love the university as a place of learning and discovery. This does not mean that university leaders should be in every case professional academics, though that qualification will be generally desirable. It is necessary, however, that the university mission be embraced with passion and dedication.

That is a vital requirement, of course, because from the perspective of a corporate leadership culture universities are entirely maddening. (Business leaders who become business school deans regularly report this.) As an organization, the university is, as a result of its decentralized character, generally inefficient in its decision making. Leaders in the university need a teacher's passion for learning and the consequent acceptance of the environment for leadership in this unique organizational context.

A second personal requirement is a high tolerance for

process. In a decentralized organization with overlapping and sometimes conflicting mechanisms of governance, there is seldom a simple path from a proposed change, large or small, to its actual implementation. It is necessary to regard this process of deliberation and exploration as one in which every opportunity for instruction and the exchange of views is exploited. A university leader cannot control this process, complex and often controversial, as a business executive might. Rather, the process must inevitably be seen as one in which better ideas and better outcomes are presented and advocated, and in which disagreements and conflicts of opinion are aired.

Essential to good teaching is effectiveness at communication. The essence of teaching is communication. No duty of the university leader can be regarded as more important than communication in directing processes of deliberation and in being the spokesperson and advocate for the university to its vast array of internal and external constituencies. In this present media age, an essential requirement of university leaders is that they be confident and competent communicators with a microphone or a television camera in their faces.

The communication requirement, in pedagogy and leadership, is of supreme importance. In the process of leadership selection in the university, communication looms large, even paramount, in the minds of selection committees. What a selection committee will certainly know after an extensive interview is whether a candidate is a good communicator. What will inevitably be less certain is the quality of the ideas being put forth. Thus, effective communication is a necessary requirement but does not guarantee the success of the university leader. Long and effective engagement with ideas as a teacher and researcher helps ensure that candidates are substantive and not merely glib.

Lastly, teachers as leaders of deliberative processes must have a high tolerance for criticism and dissent, for when ideas are advanced, they will likely provoke criticism, including personal criticism. Whatever an individual may say about the thickness of his or her skin, no one likes to be criticized and held up to public disregard. However, in a decentralized institution, populated by brilliant people who are armed with the weapons of academic freedom and great intellect, leaders may often find themselves the subject of intense, even bitter, criticism. The typical teacher-researcher has few experiences of being in the crossfire. The ability to face criticism and still render outcomes without regard to conflict is a major test of whether a teacher has the capacity to be a leader of the academic enterprise. In the end, the personal requirements for leadership in the university correlate closely with a range of talents particular to effective practitioners of the art of pedagogy.

## Conclusion

Let me present an illustration of what this notion of leadership as pedagogy looks like in operation. The leader in this case was our conference chair, Dave Brown, then-provost at Wake Forest. In the early 1990s, Wake Forest faced a number of important questions. As we evolved from a teaching to a teaching and research institution, the faculty required more time for research. Without compromising our instructional programs, this required hiring additional faculty. In addition, our student academic casualties were overwhelmingly in the first year. Since our admissions are selective, our guiding assumption is that we should graduate everyone we admit. We needed major changes in our first-year experience for students. Technology was presenting us, like schools everywhere, with major challenges. Uniformity and universality would be required to have a robust environment available to everyone, with the result that our academic program could realize the full benefits of technology. We were moving at different speeds in different directions in information technology across the institution.

As provost, Dave chaired a program planning group that he charged with the task of dealing comprehensively with these and other issues. Over the course of almost two years, the committee held town meetings and put forward report drafts and revisions of drafts. Since curricular charges were involved, proposals had to pass the undergraduate faculty. We had a full-blown campus discussion, complete with student demonstrations!

Since these plans required a proposed (large) tuition increase, for an entire year our board of trustees discussed these proposals and their financial implications. This was a period of rising concern about hikes in tuition—a quite specific concern of our trustees—and we had to be certain that we could afford to implement whatever plans might be adopted. Thus, an educational or pedagogical process for our trustees went on in tandem with our planning group.

In 1996, the committee proposed, the faculty passed, and the trustees adopted what we then called the "Plan for the Class of 2000." (This plan took four years to implement fully.) It involved major changes to the first-year experience, new faculty positions with no enrollment increase, and uniform universal technology. Each student would be given a personal computer as part of the cost of tuition. The trustees approved a graduated increase in tuition of $3,000 per year. This plan brought substantial and important changes across our university.

What is notable about this effort, in retrospect, is not just its successful outcomes (there were particular concerns about the board's willingness to raise tuition so dramatically) but how thorough were the processes of deliberation, discussion, and conferral. Of course, there was dissent throughout the process and at the end of it. But there were opportunities throughout the study for the university community to be involved in the discussion. Dave Brown did a masterful job as our teacher, assisted by many members of the faculty and the administration.

Though the problems and outcomes were much less significant, I would contrast the "Plan for the Class of 2000" with the process referred to earlier regarding our graphic identity. That process was flawed and in a certain sense failed because it did not provide the community the deliberation and consultation that might have engaged the community in the problem and the solution. Had our process been more deliberative, our implementation might have been even more effective and timely.

In short, our challenge then may have succeeded better had we approached this policy change as an exercise in learning that stressed, to carry the metaphor, not just lectures but discussion, with participation encouraged from each and every member of the class. Expecting—and I dare say even welcoming—the atmosphere of criticism and dissent would have produced the results characteristic of the teaching process itself: new and more adequate solutions to the issue at hand.

Ultimately, the leadership challenges presented by the unique culture and organization of the university are best addressed by the very skills—what I have called the "genius"— that most inform these distinct characteristics. These talents are, I have said, the quest for the new, the novel, and the unrecognized. All are the bedrock and foundation of the process of critical inquiry. Importantly, they are also key aspects of leadership.

The teaching that informs this notion of leadership is not "be still while I instill." The teaching I refer to is deliberative and interactive, involving mutual give and take. Administrative leadership in a university is likely to be effective if policy development and change is conceived as an exercise in teaching and learning aimed at deliberation, clarification, and selection.

And though the proposition may sound counterintuitive to university faculty, what good teachers do is a model from which university leadership can be drawn.

\* \* \*

*Several people commented on earlier drafts of this essay and deserve thanks: Dave Brown, John Anderson, Winn Legerton, Ellen Van Velsor, John Alexander, Bill Gordon, Russell Brantley, Murray Greason, Stas Preczewski, and especially Michael Strysick.*

SMITH RICHARDSON FOUNDATION FORUM, SEPTEMBER 23, 2003

# Heroes and Heroines

During a meeting in San Antonio, I chanced to visit the Alamo during the celebration of its sesquicentennial. My impression was that Texans had come to regret that national independence was ever yielded to a motley union of otherwise undistinguished states. You know that Texas pride of place! Having grown up on the Alamo story, I loved the visit and feasted on the valor and fortitude of those who died for freedom.

Back home, National Public Radio did a story on the sesquicentennial which reported the true—not the mythic—version of the Alamo. This report was based on careful scholarship and historical research. The famous Travis episode—the emotional highlight of the 1960 John Wayne film—never actually occurred. It was a complete invention. Crockett and Bowie were there, in the first place, for altogether unheroic motives. By the end of this report, the horrible truth was out. Our heroes were not heroes. Our history is not the stuff of legend. No glamour. No glory. No heroes.

The debunking of heroes and heroism, a demythologizing of our political history, has become a leading academic indoor sport. Washington did not cross the Delaware in blazing glory. To say, "Washington slept here," has altogether nonhistorical connotation. Jefferson, flaming disciple of liberty, owned slaves and spoke in a nasal, high-toned, unpleasant voice. Daniel Boone did not kill bears at a young age. The list continues, but you see the point. This revision of the history of our national past deprives us of heroines, heroes, or grandeur.

"In fourteen hundred and ninety-two, Columbus sailed the ocean blue!" used to be a tribute to heroism and bravery unparalleled. But read any of the books celebrating the quincentennial. Columbus was a wretched man whose deeds are not so much to be celebrated as decried.

This new history has been a painful lesson for me. My earliest serious reading was a series of orange-bound biographies of the youth of American notables. They were all people whose special gifts were evident even as children. They were marked by destiny for greatness. I devoured those books. When I had read all my library had, I read them again.

The formative event of my young life was World War II. It is always the War in my emotional vocabulary. We fought a holy war against evil forces. We believed our cause was just, even divine. Our leaders were heroes and saints. Their very names remain emotionally charged when I name or hear them named— Franklin Delano Roosevelt, Winston Churchill, Dwight D.

Eisenhower, Patton, MacArthur, Montgomery. Can you imagine how cruel and unwelcome have been the biographical studies of these legendary figures which have been forced upon my generation? The demythologizing goes on. John F. Kennedy and Martin Luther King have been given the same scorching treatment by the spotlight of objective, scholarly, historical research.

The movies (there was a time before TV, though students are unwilling to believe that anyone now living could have personally witnessed such a remote and dismal world. "What did you do without TV?" one of my children asked in disbelief) reinforced our disposition to idolatry, heroism, and legend. There were the war movies and westerns, of course, all morality plays in which the righteous were victorious. But the films of this period, on all subjects, provided food for this appetite for splendid events acted out by people of dedication, devotion, and brilliance. I see these films occasionally now in the company of student audiences at the campus film series. Audience reaction is painful. Student audiences see these films as comic, even ludicrous parodies of the real. For the audiences for whom they were made—long ago and even further away—these stories were the stuff of dreams and dreamers.

Sport was another heroic preoccupation of my young life. Here was another scene of dramatic and heroic endeavor. Joe DiMaggio, Bob Feller (he was my favorite baseball player; I yearned to be a pitcher), Jackie Robinson, and Joe Lewis performed feats of superhuman proportions. Superman was born of this era. In the 1960's when Simon and Garfunkel sang, "Where have you gone Joe DiMaggio? Joltin' Joe has left and gone away!" we all knew the meaning of that departure—the death of heroes.

Political leaders cannot be heroes or heroines. They now engage in the public character assassination and vilification of each other, which demeans them all. "Political hero" is an oxymoron. Political candidacy has less to do with governing than with television, a miniseries or soap opera with unsavory stories and characters.

There was a view of history in this idolatry we practiced, perhaps even a view of life itself. Human events are in the hands of a few great people of great achievement who, as Shakespeare said of Caesar, "bestride the narrow world like a colossus." It was part of my well-schooled idolatry that these special people were of great moral and intellectual stature. They led because they were gifted and dedicated to ideal purposes. Why does that view now seem so simplistic and naive?

I have regretted, even resented, the loss of my heroes. It has impoverished my soul. I regret this loss for students. How do we educate and inspire without models of rectitude, measures of achievement? Are not heroes and heroines the very stuff of idealism? Are the young not to be given ideals? Are they not to have a reach beyond their grasp? If you see the "most admired by college students" list, it is dominated by entertainers. What is worse, it is dominated by entertainers I have never heard of.

Yes, Joe DiMaggio is gone. Objects of veneration are nowhere to be found. Historical figures? The truth is now in print. Political leaders? Never. Sports figures? They are on strike. Joe never played for money, did he?

I search here for a saving grace. Perhaps we do well not to be so completely given to hero worship. To make too much of the achievements of others is to undervalue our own possibilities. To divide the world neatly into the gifted few and the ordinary many is to say that destiny for most of us is limited and closed.

The many—you and I—might be free to do then a lesser bidding, to merely stand and wait in the service of greatness. There is thus this lesson, offered as cold consolation to those of us who mourn the passing of the age of veneration: the human potential of any, even the least of us, is as high as our dreams and as wide as our doings.

# *Leadership*

L eadership has been called the most observed and least understood phenomenon in human society. The effort to improve our understanding is now fully underway. Indeed, the subject shows all the signs of becoming trendy, so much so that we can predict a *Time* cover before long, a signal that interest in leadership has peaked and will soon be on the wane. It was not always so. James MacGregor Burns reports that in the late sixties when he was researching his book, *Leadership*, the best work on the subject to date, there was no entry in the New York Public Library under this heading.

One reason, of course, that the subject was not studied and taught systematically until recently. The legacy of the traditions of the nineteenth century regarded leadership as a charismatic gift, something incapable of analysis or description. Much of the history of our century seemed to confirm the belief that leadership simply appeared in the world and exercised its influence for good or ill, but like the other gifts of prophecy, it could not be directed or influenced. How could one explain the presence of Hitler, Lenin, or Stalin on history's center stage except that these men had an inexplicable gift of charismatic leadership?

Thanks to the labor of Burns and others, and to a growing understanding of group behavior, there is consensus that the subject of leadership can be understood in a way that permits the subject to occupy the importance the topic requires. Even scant experience will convince most people that the quality of leadership, as much as any single factor, will determine the success of any collective undertaking. Plans, resources, and technologies will often not suffice to achieve a collective outcome in the absence of effective leadership. If leadership occupies this critical role in the social process, then few subjects are more important for our consideration.

The first lesson in understanding leadership requires that we dismiss the notion that there are singular characteristics that separate leaders from followers. Leaders, like followers, come in many shapes and sizes. The second point is that leadership should be seen as relational; it concerns a functional relationship between individuals and groups. The dynamics of the leadership process owe as much to the character of the group as to the leaders. As there are infinite numbers of groups and personalities of leaders in those groups, the subject is much more complex than the simple enumeration of a set of traits of people thought to be leaders.

Think for a moment of all the groups you participate in

and all the people who exercise leadership in those groups, and your own experience will reveal the complexity of the subject. This complexity has a positive outcome for the study of leadership, however. Our task is not merely to identify a set of characteristics had by a few people. It is, rather, to better understand the relationships between leaders and groups in the belief that the leadership capacities of both individuals and groups can be enhanced by understanding and effort.

A first lesson in leadership then is that the study is relational; it concerns the dynamics of interaction between individuals, leaders, and groups. Statements of the "characteristics" of leaders, abstracted from relations to groups led, will inevitably omit at least half the equation of leadership. It is thus vital that the study of leadership be situational, that it reflect the situation of the group or organization. Leadership is not, on this analysis, a neutral force to be exercised in the same way in any group at any point in its history. Groups need and will permit leadership according to their own history, needs, and opportunities.

Organizations differ radically in terms of both history and function. I worry that leadership studies will suffer from too close an identification with business schools where much important work in this field is being done. Business leadership will not, despite a common prejudice to the contrary, transfer without loss to the realms of politics, education, or the volunteer sector where leadership must take often a very different character. Even organizations of the same type require and will permit very different leadership, depending on the problems being faced or the group's experience with previous leadership.

Leadership study thus must reflect situational or organizational analysis as well as the relational features of group and leader interaction.

These points are often expressed in abstract language but are meant to reflect common sense and practice. When an organization sets out to choose a leader, either by an election or something so formal as a professional search, the first thing to determine is the present needs of the organization in terms of which group's leadership requirements can be formulated. Candidates for public office regularly tell us what our problems are and why they are the leader best suited to address those particular issues. Implicitly or not, leadership choice does (or should) involve situational analysis.

What can be generally described, in terms relevant to almost any group of any size or purpose, are the formal tasks of leaders, what it is that leaders do in and for the groups they lead. These formal tasks, if well done, maximize the group's chances for success in its collective undertakings. Nothing can guarantee that the group will succeed, of course. It may fail for any number of reasons despite superior leadership efforts. A company with the best leadership may face economic circumstances that cause it to fail despite all.

The first formal task of leadership in a group is to secure adequate planning. No group can function effectively lacking a sense of direction, knowledge of purpose, and strategies for how they might be achieved and maintained. This may be something as grand as a transformational vision describing how an organization can become, in the future, something grander than it has been. At the other extreme, an organization may have no purpose beyond a monthly meeting for the entertainment of its members, in which case the planning task is modest but still essential. This formal task of planning can be accomplished in many ways, depending on the character of both the leader and the group. For most groups, plans must analyze what problems must be solved and which opportunities exploited for the group to achieve its collective aims. If the group aims are complex, the plans will be also. The leader sees that the plan is suitable to the purposes the group envisions. The prophet Isaiah said, "Where there is no vision, the people perish." In humbler terms, where there is no plan, groups do not know what they are doing. Leadership must see that there is a plan that grows from the group purpose which provides direction and promises progress toward collective goals.

The next and equally important task of leadership is the communication of this plan to the group. If it is a grand vision of a prophet or teacher or the simple plan for a book club, the plan must be shared to guide group behavior. Again, there are many styles and ways in which the plan can be communicated so that it may form the basis of collective action. The more complicated the group and its plans, the more difficult the communicative task becomes. I call this the pedagogical task of leadership.

Unless the plan is effectively shared, it fulfills no purpose. At its best, the group internally appropriates the plan and it serves to unite and strengthen the group's sense of identity. That process can make it possible to achieve in the group those higher levels of voluntary commitment, which are frequently the difference between success and failure.

My thesis is that these are the two indispensable tasks of leaders in organizations. Of course, many leaders are chosen who fail in these tasks. To occupy a position of leadership is not to lead. In larger organizations, these tasks become complex, and to these tasks must be added a third: to see that other leadership is provided. If this summary is correct, the conclusion follows that these formal tasks of leadership are teachable. These skills of planning and communication are matters that people can learn to perform. Again, how they are done will depend on all those factors we have considered: the leader, the group, and the situation. Depending on the nature and complexity of the group, these tasks will be easier or harder. Leaders will need appropriate training, depending on the groups in which leadership is to be exercised. The conclusion of most importance, however, is that leadership can be developed. It does not depend upon the discovery of those rare people—who do exist of course—with innate, charismatic gifts. The teaching of leadership is, at bottom, amazingly simple and easy: people who lead must be taught to plan and to communicate. The leadership capability of almost anyone is there to be realized.

Leaders are for the most part made, not born.

# *Leadership in Higher Education*

Most academic leadership is drawn from the ranks of the faculty. Faculty attitudes are important, therefore, in forming the administrative ideas of deans, vice presidents, and presidents. Faculty attitudes about administration are generally negative. These faculty attitudes are not often discussed seriously, but they form a serious policy issue for university leadership.

These negative attitudes have several important sources. Faculty members are a highly intelligent and naturally critical group. Their work is problem solving and the sustained criticism of proposed solutions. In their primary professional roles, faculty members are all but autonomous. Therefore, where faulty work is intersected by administrative decisions about space, resources, or staff, faculty naturally regard such intrusions with the same tools of criticism they use in their disciplines.

The faculty carries out the fundamental work of the university. The administration exists mainly to facilitate the work of the faculty and students. In a peculiar twist on an old adage, "Those who can, teach; those who can't, go into administration." The order of priority that emerges from the natural purpose of the university places the faculty above the administration. However, institutional leaders occupy positions of control, which determine the success or failure of faculty initiatives.

There is a common view among faculty members that anyone of reasonable intelligence can do the work of the administration. (A fellow president once remarked, "Half of my faculty think they can do my job as well as I can. The other half think anyone could do as well.") The intellectual requirements of institutional management are not extraordinary. But the intellectual gifts are not primary in academic administration. As in all leadership roles, the difficult and perplexing issues arise out of the ongoing effort to identify the primary problems and opportunities of the institution, and to marshal the resources of the institution to solve its problems and exploit its opportunities. The primary problems are human problems. Being smart is not sufficient to be an educational leader or manager.

The university is a complex organism, composed of many groups of groups. These groups have interests that sometimes coincide, but more often they conflict. Bringing guidance and consensus to these conflicts is a difficult exercise in institutional leadership. Allocating scarce resources across these groups generally means that respect, let alone popularity, is an elusive goal for institutional leaders. Many common tools of inquiry in the disciplines of the academy cast issues into a problem of class conflict, power, and politics. To these faculty, there is an inevitable and sometimes adversarial conflict among groups in the university.

People are drawn to university life in the first instance because of commitment to ideas. The natural inclination and temperament of the faculty, therefore, does not direct them toward administrative or organizational concerns. The initial talent pool for institutional leadership is smaller than in other organizations.

Within the university, there are relatively few opportunities for young faculty to determine whether they have administrative interest and aptitude. The opportunities to chair major committees or serve as department heads are given to senior colleagues. Many gifted leaders simply never have an opportunity to test their talent and interest.

Because communication skills play an important role both in the classroom and in administration, good teachers are often chosen for administrative positions. There is certainly a basis for that selection. But while communication skills are necessary, they are far from sufficient for success in the larger task of academic leadership. Universities tend to overselect for these skills to the neglect of other important leadership qualities. Style is no substitute for substance.

The modern university has become a complex and complicated institution. Its reach extends not only to intellectual and academic organizations, but to city, state, and federal governments, local community groups, philanthropic organizations, athletic clubs, alumni groups, and the list goes on. Managing these vital and important institutions is a noble calling. The university, so skilled at providing leadership for every other sector of society, needs to attend to its own leadership demands. It makes a difference.

# Why Americans
# Hate Politics

My friend, Russell, gave me a book one Christmas entitled *Why Americans Hate Politics*. It was a thoughtful, sober analysis of the contemporary American political scene.

*The central argument of this book is liberalism
and conservatism are framing political issues as
a series of false choices.
Wracked by contradiction and responsive
mainly to the needs of their constituencies,
liberalism and conservatism prevent the nation
from settling the questions that most trouble it.*

*On issue after issue, there is consensus on where*

*the nation should move or at least on what we*

*should be arguing about; liberalism and*

*conservatism make it impossible for that*

*consensus to express itself.*

E. J. DIONNE

As I read it, however, I liked the title better than the book. I do not know whether Americans hate politics, but I do. The title became an epiphany of sorts for me. This represents an enormous change in my attitude. I have always been a seriously interested citizen—watching the conventions, reading political commentaries, and working in various campaigns of both parties across the years. This year, I could not watch the candidates or the pundits. I watched not a minute of either convention and almost none of the debates. I, a true-blue citizen, found that I hated politics. Why?

One reason Americans hate politics is because there is too much of it. Elections seem never to stop. Members of the House of Representatives are always running for office. As soon as one presidential election is over, the other starts. There seems no relief from it, so Americans are overdosed on politics, and I, for one, am sick of it.

There is a deeper reason for my distaste of politics, however. Politics is roughly defined as the art of government. In our society, however, politics has lost any relationship with the governing of the country. That is why I hate the process. Ostensibly, politics is about the management of the country. In fact, it has no relationship with government at all.

This came to me suddenly when I was listening one morning to Cokie Roberts, one of my favorite public commentators. She was talking about the political process, but her language made it appear that she was talking about a dramatic series. She talked about a "plot" that had to be played out. She referred to characters that had to be developed. She discussed various "dramatic themes" which will be considered. Suddenly, it struck me. This is not about government. This is about a television miniseries. If there were any doubt about the matter, just look at what the political conventions have become. They have no relationship to the government, nor do they have any real relationship to the choosing of a candidate. They are a media show put on for the benefit of the television. I came to realize in a flash, politics is not about government. It is about television. The issue for politicians is not how things are, in fact, or what the country's policies might be or should be. The question is how they appear on television. Thus, my distaste for politics. It is ostensibly about the government. It is, in fact, about television. Television is about images and appearances. It is about raising money for advertising. It is about enhancing thereby the power of the PACS.

It is about quotable phrases and sound bites and focus groups. The phrases that I remember from this current political season are the following: "Give America back to the people,"

"Get this country moving again," "Put America back to work," "Make this country great again." This may be the stuff of a miniseries. It has little relationship to what the needs of the country are in the world.

Perhaps the ill-fated campaign of Ross Perot came to this. He believed that the process of running for office was about governing the country. When he hired professional campaign managers, they told him that it was about opinion polls, interest groups, and television. He quit in disgust. I, for one, do not blame him.

Advertising is television's most characteristic presentation. As politics has become a media show, the emphasis on packaging candidates and their messages so that they play well on the media has become fundamental. Candidates do not and should not be expected to have real political beliefs. They must put forward those images that play well to various interest groups. In the 1992 election, we read that the Democrats are struggling to regain former voters recently drawn to the Republicans by conservative themes; thus, Clinton and Gore give us conservative messages. Are they conservatives? No one knows. What is more, no one even cares. This process is about politics, not about government.

The prominence of abortion in the current political discussion is evidence of our political malaise. It is an issue made for TV, complete with dramatic visuals. It is very divisive and polarizing. It bears on the future of the country hardly at all but is the kind of politics that the media engenders.

On a more substantive level, everyone knows that the major problems of this country cannot be addressed without pain. I recall the words of Winston Churchill: "I have nothing to offer you except blood, sweat, toil, and tears." The message now is taken straight from the advertising room: all will be sweetness, light, and harmony. There are no challenges that the election of this or that person will not remedy.

Governing the country is about the substance of our lives and of the lives of people around the world. How tragic it is that the political process in this country now forbids that we ask and answer the hard questions that will shape our future and the future of our children.

# Leadership:
# Transforming Organizations

About a dozen years ago now I had an experience of illumination, the kind of moment literary people call an "epiphany." Since that experience explains my presence and my subject here today, perhaps you will indulge this bit of intellectual autobiography.

My university was in a difficult financial and administrative period. "Crisis" is too strong a term, but things seemed critical to me at the time. I was sitting in my office late one afternoon, my feet propped up on the desk, looking out the window, pondering my woes.

Two groups of reports from my units were in front of me proposing financial and personnel remedies. One group had responded effectively. The other group gave evidence of indecision and, worse, efforts at buck passing. The thought suddenly crossed my mind that the difference between the two stacks was simple. The first group of units had good leadership. The second group did not. That reflection led to another which struck me vividly: my primary job as an academic administrator was leadership development.

I have no idea why that thought struck me with such force, but it startled me, and I was sure from that very moment that this intuition was important and would change my view of educational administration. I remember thinking that no one I could recall had discussed the subject of leadership in my presence since Boy Scout days. If leadership was my primary job, why had no one ever mentioned that to me? Why had I been so slow to realize it?

My first responsibility was to inform myself. Like a good academic, I went to the library, checked out everything I could find, and started reading. I read a long list of titles before I discovered James MacGregor Burn's *Leadership*, a rich and complex study that remains one of the important books of my life. We had Professor Burns on campus last spring, and I was able to acknowledge my debt to his work. Best of all, his visit provided us a long conversation about leadership.

In this same period, a group in Birmingham was formed out of shared civic concerns. From our meetings emerged a community leadership organization, Leadership Birmingham, which has become a positive influence in that city. My first civic undertaking when I came to Wake Forest was the establishment of Leadership Winston-Salem. My sojourn with leadership issues started with my vocation, in which my conception of my task was changed, and became a primary commitment of my civic life.

The journey with leadership is not finished, however. At Wake Forest we are determining what leadership studies should mean for our university. We have a number of emerging programs devoted to the recruitment, recognition, and training of leaders among Wake Forest students. I hope that leadership will become one of the primary interests and emphases of our university.

My first studies on leadership were disappointing. There is a strong nineteenth century tradition of leadership theory that emphasized the role of "charismatic" leaders, the "great man" theory of leadership which reflects a larger view of history. On this view, leaders are born, not made. Our century has seemed to vindicate this nonrational or suprarational view of leadership development. Hitler, Mussolini, Lenin, and Stalin all seemed to illustrate the idea that leadership, for good or ill, is simply a gift. In Burns, however, I found an alternative framework for understanding this subject, which made the subject amenable to study in theory and practice.

I propose three simple truths about leadership. If you can take these from this gathering, you will have a summary of my reflections since that day the subject presented itself to me. First, the key to the success of any organization, no matter how large or small, is leadership. Plans, resources, technology, and every other organizational requirement can be present in abundance. Given every other asset, organizations are unlikely to make progress in the absence of leadership. Leadership makes successful collective undertakings possible. Leadership does not guarantee success, of course, only the possibility of success. This maxim is a summary of my own experience and is coming to be recognized generally in organizational study.

The views that I present here are not those of Burns. His work is rich and complex, not for leisure reading. My views have been formed largely by reading and thinking through his analyses. Second, the skills and talents of leadership are largely acquirable. While there are doubtless natural leaders, people with gifts in the relevant areas, what is required for individuals to move organizations is teachable and learnable. The tradition of the charismatic leader is not the whole story. There is a discipline and a set of skills to be applied that make the subject proper for study and research. Leadership can be developed in individuals and groups.

Third, the primary test and task of leadership is the development of other leadership. It is not enough that an organization have a leader. Too much thinking about leadership has focused on the individual leader rather than the corporate collective leadership needs of organizations and groups. If leadership is the key ingredient of organizational development, the leader must expand this indispensable resource, as John Kotter notes in *The Leadership Factor*. That was what I realized that afternoon. If I had done my job in leadership development, all my units would have had people ready to deal with the trials of the moment. Surprisingly, many gifted leaders fail to develop the skills and talents in those around them.

These elements of leadership theory and practice are at last beginning to be heard. There is growing interest in this subject in and out of university settings. Publications are appearing, and institutes and centers are being formed. All these are important and positive developments.

## Leadership Studies

The study of leadership involves understanding three components of an organization's life. Such an analysis differs for each organization. Leadership analysis is dependent on the organizational or institutional context. These three are: (1) the leader and leadership needs; (2) the followership needs of the group and human resources of the organization; and (3) the organizational context, the history, circumstances and prospects of the organization. The exercise of leadership must reflect these essential elements. A person can be a great leader, but if there is not effective relationship to the group and its circumstances, there will be no followers.

Leaders are different. Followers are different. Organizations are different. There must be consistency and convergence among these elements, and all must be taken into account. Leadership is not some neutral force to be employed at any time in any group in the same way. Leadership analysis is situational and circumstantial. The notion that the leader arrives new on the scene and starts immediately to lead reflects a dangerous, often disastrous misconception. The leader will first listen and learn unless the organization is in profound crisis. A leader is a learner. The leader—and this is trivial but profoundly true—leads the group. Leadership is relational.

Leadership involves a relationship between the leader and the needs and circumstances of the group led. There is no leadership without followership. There was a cartoon showing a befuddled army officer seeking directions at a rural store. The caption reads: "Where is my regiment? I must find them. I am their leader." There are many would-be leaders whose followers have long since gone.

It follows, of course, that leadership does not occur merely because someone is in a position of leadership. People are given positions and fail to lead. Leadership is not always exercised by presidents or chairmen. The question of organizational leadership is not a matter of title. It concerns the actual exercise of influence in the group. Informal organizational structures defy organizational charts, and real—rather than titular—influence is found in those holding no formal title. There is power behind the throne. People in positions to lead are most in need of reflective understanding of that responsibility. To hold office is not to lead.

This relational view means that a leader is to be contrasted with a tyrant. Merely to exercise power is not to lead. A tyrant uses a group to achieve ends that may not be in the best interest of the group. The leader is committed to the enhancement of the enlightened interests of the group. Tyrants, like terrorists, have power, but they do not lead. Leaders exercise power that is legitimate. In terms of political theory, leaders have authority, not merely power. The influence of leadership is sanctioned formally or informally by the group. Merely to exercise coercion of any sort—economic or force of arms—is not to lead. Leaders are not tyrants, and that is more than a semantic distinction.

Leaders come in all sorts of personalities and styles. This belies the notion that there is a certain personality that goes with being a leader. Think of all the groups you know and the varieties of people who lead them. There are quiet leaders, forceful leaders, stubborn leaders, and wise leaders. There is leadership from the front and from the rear.

The task of leadership, education, and development is to assist people to develop their unique strengths. The task of leadership is not simply to wait for the arrival of a person with charisma. Not all leaders are of the charismatic sort, and that leadership style would be ill-adapted to many, perhaps most, organizations.

The key to Burns' analysis of leadership is the distinction between transactional and transformational change in organizations, and hence between transactional and transformational leadership. I have adapted his terminology for my own purposes. Transactional leadership concerns the managerial, organizational, administrative, and bureaucratic life of an organization. At this level, the leader transacts the business of the group, and acts to direct and execute the collective outcomes of group deliberation.

It is common now to distinguish between managers and leaders. If that is a useful distinction, the manager acts transactionally. We should not, however, denigrate the management function or fail to give transactional leadership the regard it is due. An organization with effective transactional leadership is blessed. In transactional leadership, there is a close convergence between the leader and the group led. This kind of leadership is what many organizations want and need. It is what many organizations will tolerate. The transactional manager represents a vital organizational resource. In complex organizations, transactional skills are needed at every level of structure.

In transformational leadership, by contrast, the group is changed, transformed by the initiative of the leader. Rather than directing the leader's activities, the group accepts a new role and mission as a result of the transformational leader's influence. Transformational leaders remake organizations and lift their levels of aspiration and achievement. In this process of transformational leadership is contained much of our hope for human social, political, and economic progress. If groups are to lift their level of achievement, that enhancement requires the influence of transformational leaders.

Leadership discussions are complicated because we often cannot describe examples of common agreement. Best-known leaders are in politics, but we do not often agree on leadership capacity. (How do you stand on Harry Truman or Dwight D. Eisenhower as leaders?) At this meeting, however, we have been fortunate to hear a transformational leader, Fred Smith of Federal Express. I need not search further for illustration. I want to use his presentations as concrete examples of the theory of leadership I am advancing. His presentations illustrate what is central to the achievement of transformational leadership.

The first task of transformational leadership is to cast a vision of the organization's future possibility. To quote from the prophet Isaiah, "Where there is no vision the people perish." A transformational leader sets forth the vision, dreams the dream.

If you attended Fred Smith's session on personnel management, his first words were about vision. Personnel management does not begin with salary, fringe benefits, and the like. In the first instance, people are invited to share a vision of the company's opportunities and prospects. Before there is the real, there is the conception of the possible. Before the real, there is the what might be. If you went to hear a talk on personnel issues, would you expect to hear about corporate vision? You would if the speaker is a transformational leader.

Transformational leaders, prophets, and reformers are those who move the world's collective enterprises forward. That progress begins with the casting of a dream of the sort Fred Smith had about air express opportunities. To have that vision is the first and foremost task of the leader. Almost everything else the transformational leader does is coincidental to the vision. It is the motivating force of group achievement.

Put another way, the first task of leadership is planning. The word "planning" is perhaps too neutral to describe this visionary casting, but it emphasizes that transformational leadership is projective and prospective. In any organization, people will bemoan yesterday and worry about today unless the leader points at tomorrow. Planning is the process by which the leader's vision is rendered specific. The leader's goal or vision must be translated into plans and plans into strategies and the formulation of options. The leader is a planner.

The leader will bring to the process of planning the best minds to be found. People with fresh perspective and novel ideas will be sought out. Above all, the leader will regard planning as a participatory exercise so that those charged with carrying out the vision will participate in its formation. If the vision is to have motivating influence over the entire group, it must be shared.

Almost equal in importance is that the transformational vision must be given voice. The vision and the plans must be shared. They must be appropriated so that they are for the group, not just for the leader. A plan, no matter how visionary, will never transform unless it is given voice. The sharing and communication of the vision can be regarded as a kind of transformational teaching. The leader has a primary teaching function if the vision is to become that of the group. The transformational leader is thus planner and teacher.

You must have been struck by Fred Smith's powers of communication. He visibly demonstrated his capacity to share his ideas with people. His goals are clear, and his commitment and enthusiasm for his company are contagious. His vision has a voice. He teaches. He has learned to extend his voice through the remarkable networks of communication his company has created. He has adopted the best technologies to see that people hear, see, and feel the influence of the company's goals. It is not just Fred Smith who speaks. It is Federal Express. His vision is the vision of its employees. This is corporate leadership at its best.

Many styles of communication are effective. One need not be effective in public forums as Fred Smith is. One important leader in my community makes no public speeches at all. He is, however, a remarkable communicator in small groups or one-on-one. Whatever the style of communication, a transformational leader must communicate his vision and energy to the group. A vision without voice is empty. It will gain no adherents, no transforming energy.

Winston Churchill said that in World War II he was not the British lion, but he was the roar. That roar was indispensable to victory. Communication skills are highly valued in organizations. My experience suggests that such skills are probably overvalued and over selected. They are quickly discernable in interviews, and good communicators will be sought by headhunters. People can be given leadership positions because they can communicate, but many fail as transformational leaders because they have no insight or vision. It is not enough to be glib or charming. Because something waddles, quacks, and swims, it may not yet be a duck.

Many people who look, sound, and act like leaders are not. Transformational leaders must have vision first and second give voice to that vision. Without vision, the voice is empty. Groups will listen for a while to an effective communicator. Absent the vision, there will ultimately be no followership. Communication skills are powerful instruments of group change. They are also acquirable with desire and effort, but these skills are futile without the imagination and intellect to see an enlarged future.

Any organization has two elements. One, the products, services, structure, finance, and technology. And two, the people who provide, produce, or deliver the services. The leader knows that people come first, last, and always. Leadership will emphasize human resources as the fundamental institutional asset.

I can do no better than quote Fred Smith. "People first;

people before profits," he said. He commented on the large amounts of his time given to personnel matters. Fred Smith knows that people build great organizations. Leaders build people and multiply human resources. Leaders will seek to multiply and enhance leadership talent. Therefore, Federal Express has established a leadership institute for this purpose. It is not, he was at pains to say, a management training center. Its business is leadership development. Fred Smith has learned this essential lesson of organizational success. Any person can be taught to put human resources first in an order of priority.

When a transformational leader finds other leaders, they are trained and empowered. A transformational leader knows how to trust and reward them. The leader knows that to focus on the human resources of the group will require delegation of the functional tasks of the organization. Many fail to lead by giving primary, often expert, concern to matters other than human development.

As an aside, I believe that the MBA programs of our nation are beginning to learn these lessons. After years of primary emphasis on the fiscal and analytic side of business development, business educators are turning to the human resource issues in organizational development. It is not enough to learn the technical elements of financial analysis. More thorough management of existing assets will never transform. The Broyhill family—of North Carolina furniture fame—has established a chair in Wake Forest's Babcock Graduate School of Management devoted to leadership development study. Our MBA students participate in Outward Bound.

There are personal requirements that enhance the effectiveness of transformational leadership. I hesitate at this point because I stress that leaders are different. But there are facilitating characteristics. Above all, leaders exhibit persistence and determination. Woody Allen (noted organizational theorist!) said that ninety percent of success is showing up. Leaders show up. There is a fundamental fact here. People do not work hard because they are leaders; they are leaders because they work hard. Groups learn quickly which individuals can be counted on. When someone successfully carries out a task, the group assigns them another. The process continues. Leaders get things done because they work at it. Persistence is part of the same equation. Leaders do not yield in the presence of obstacles. They have the staying power that any complex achievement requires.

———————————

YOUNG PRESIDENTS ORGANIZATION, BERMUDA
JUNE 23, 1988

# PUBLIC ADDRESSES

# Lessons in
# Podium Etiquette

Giving major public presentations involves more than meets the eye. In the interest of better understanding these important occasions, I'd like to offer the following observations. Most of the time, there is a printed program with a published title, which is a serious problem right there. The program goes to print weeks before the speech is written. The first lesson for speaker and audience is to disregard the title. "Issues for the 1990s" is a great title because it takes up about the right amount of space in the program and permits a speech on any subject whatsoever.

In the old days, important speeches were called orations. The only place that title survives is at Wake Forest University, where selected seniors give orations at commencement ceremonies. There are a lot of problems with orations, which is why they have all but disappeared. Technically speaking, orations should be in Latin. This was hard on some listeners, of course, but worse for speakers. Latin is a dead language, which means that we do not know how it is pronounced.

I made the mistake once of raising this pronunciation issue with my Latin teacher in the middle of a Latin recitation. He had an ingenious and instant reply: Julius Caesar, he said, came to him in his dreams, and they conversed in Latin. That is how he knew. I knew better than to argue with a man whose grasp included not only Latin pronunciation but the grade book. Orations are out.

It matters what the program says right before the title. Is this an "address" or a "speech"? An address is formal and must have a complete text, last for at least twenty minutes, and close with some flowery language at the end. While not essential, it helps if an address has a good idea or two. The idea part can, of course, be overdone, especially if you're speaking to an audience that has had a long day concluding with a cocktail party and a heavy dinner followed by the address. In these circumstances, the address need not entertain, or even awaken, the audience.

A speech is less formal than an address. For example, an address contains only the politest of humor, but a speech permits considerable comic leeway. Indeed, a joke or two, no matter how shopworn, is *de rigueur* to convince the audience that the speaker has a sense of humor. Audiences are trained in the proper response to the afterdinner speech. They pay attention to the jokes before nodding off only when the subject of the speech finally comes up. It is important that the speaker not drop a joke in the middle. Nothing is worse than a joke when no one is awake to laugh.

For both addresses and speeches, a formal introduction is mandatory. Quite often, the speaker is well-known to the audience. Even so, the speaker "who needs no introduction" gets one. The safest introduction is one that the speaker writes themself. The speaker's office can also provide a short bio suitable for reading, but this safe course of action is seldom followed, however. The introducer is, after all, simply giving a speech (or an address) about the speaker. This can be dangerous. On one occasion, I was introduced by someone who could recall everything about me but my name. The head table looked as if the introduction had become an invocation. There is always the chance that the introducer will upstage the speaker, but this is more likely to happen when the introducer goes off-subject and instead of introducing the speaker proceeds to give most of the speaker's content.

There are other less forbidding public appearances. "Talks" do not amount to much and can be delivered casually from notes. Talks, like "remarks," are meant to signal to the speaker the most important element of his presentation: brevity. I was given a warm and lengthy introduction to a faculty which ended by saying I was on the program to give word of welcome!

# Visions and Dreams

Wordsworth wrote of the river of his boyhood:

*That one, the fairest of all rivers, loved*
*To blend his murmurs with my nurse's song,*
*And from his alder shades and rocky falls,*
*And from his fords and shallows,*
*Sent a voice that flowed along my dreams?*

This river, your river, the Tennessee, blended his murmurs with my mother's song and sent a voice with me that has flowed through all my dreams. How wonderful it is to be in the Tennessee River Valley and to see the green, green hills of home. No matter where our paths may lead us, the lure of home is strong. Being here nourishes my soul and I am grateful for this occasion.

Though our family lived on Sand Mountain, the river was where we went for fun and frolic, and the sounds and sights of the river are always associated with those innocent and joyful days. Since my brother Joel grew up to be a river rat, the opportunity is given me to visit from time to time. I am always glad to be among the Tennessee River's shades and falls, and fords and shallows. This is the place of the dreams of childhood.

Growing up in Albertville, and now having lived my life in the academy, caused me at an earlier stage to wish that I had been given as a youth more culturally advantaged opportunity. It would have been well, I used to think, to have traveled and to have lived where there was regular engagement with culture. I now know the folly of that notion. Growing up in a small hill town was a childhood of the most ideal sort. We were safe. We were free—the only rule was to be home by dark.

We were surrounded by a large and loving extended family. Everywhere we were taught the prophet's law—to do justice, to love mercy, and to walk humbly with God. But, most of all, we were encouraged to believe that all our dreams could come true. No better experience for a child is possible. There may be those of you here who have had childhoods in small towns, or on farms which have provided you qualities of experience and opportunities which you may have yet to recognize.

Home is people, of course, as well as place. I am honored that my mother and many of those nearest and dearest to me have come to make this a homecoming in the complete sense. I admit as well to some anxiety about those familiar faces in this audience. Joel called recently to tell me that this speech had to be, in a term he reserves for highest praise, "a classic," and, thus, by implication, not my usual offering. The wisdom that a prophet has no honor in his own country goes double for one's own family. "Classic," indeed! Who does he think I am? Abraham Lincoln? Winston Churchill?

I am also delighted to be at the University of North Alabama. I have known your president since my days in the University of Alabama system. He has enjoyed a distinguished and remarkable tenure. Growing enrollments, new programs and facilities promise that UNA will be a school of expanding service and opportunity.

Your university's growth will be fueled by the progress of the new South. The Olympics having been held in Atlanta was an historic symbol of the new status of this region in the nation and the world. The rate of economic development of the southeast is leading the rest of the nation, and that growth promises to accelerate into the new century. Alabama has yet to participate in this emerging south to the degree that its people and potential deserve. Politically, economically, and educationally, Alabama is an unfinished work. With this economic engine heading in your direction, and with institutions like this one giving you the requisite skills for the creation of a better future, this will be an extraordinary period of opportunity for this student generation. This state needs you. You must be prepared to lead Alabama and the region into a new and better place within these United States and the world.

Well, as a native son returning, what gift of words can I

bring? I have decided to tell you what I most deeply believe about education, having devoted my life to this enterprise. And because education is not just my profession, but my passion, I will be also telling my family why my life has been so fortunate and fulfilled. I have been able to do with my life what I most wanted to do. I have lived my dream. My message to you is to make your dream become your lives. That possibility is what I most deeply believe about the promises of education.

Here we are at the opening of school in the year of our Lord 1998. Those of you enrolled here at UNA have been going to school for a long time. Much that was valuable, I am sure, preceded your attendance at UNA, in grammar school, middle school, and high school. For many, however, vital and essential things are often lost in school. Going to school over twelve years or more becomes routine—an often dreaded and dull routine at that. We seek the easiest ways out. We decide we do not like or are not good in certain subjects. We learn that some teachers are easy or indifferent. We often end up doing as little as possible to achieve whatever our limited goals may be. Challenge becomes a thing to avoid. School, we decide, is ordinary at best and dreadful at worst. So many students arrive at college with few expectations except for more schooling, and few ambitions except to get it over with and get a job.

Life happens. Problems intervene which limit our opportunities and choices. Adolescence happens with its terrifying life changes. We experiment with alcohol and drugs. Illness strikes. Given all that can and does happen, a world that once seemed to the child to contain every possibility suddenly seems limited and closed.

We arrive here, having done a lot of schooling, much of it unsatisfying. And most of all, we think we know what education is. Education is about admissions, courses, prerequisites, requirements, grades, term papers, examinations, credit hours, class preparations and presentations, and on and on. Or, at a slightly more exalted level, it is about some job opportunity you seek for yourself—being an accountant, or a teacher, or an administrator.

This is what I most believe about education. Education involves such matters, but it is not about courses or grades. College is about your dreams. In college, you have a rich and never-to-be-repeated opportunity to give your dreams the substance of ambition, and to acquire the skills and capacities to have your ambitions become your lives. Most come expecting too little, and too little is achieved. Education is the stuff of dreams. Our dreams through education are given shape into ambition, and the dream provides the passion whereby the ambition can be realized in the world.

The prophet Joel—the Old Testament one, not to be confused with my brother—said that the Lord would pour out his spirit upon the people, and that the young men and women would dream dreams and see visions. At its heart, that is what education at UNA is about. My gift of words is to urge you to pursue your dream. Though your dream may seem to have been lost to life or, tragically, to school, you have been given today a new opportunity. College makes it possible for us to reinvent ourselves, to recreate our vision for what our lives may be. It is not too late. Do not settle for going to school. School is a place and process. Education is a state of mind in which your highest and noblest purposes for your life can be transformed into livable ambitions. This transforming process happens on campuses across America and is here for you at UNA.

I hope that you meet one of those fortunates here at UNA with your dreams in your head and heart and you are engaged now in making your dreams into ambition. But all my experience confirms that you are the fortunate few. Most of you are here to be in school to get a degree and a job. You doubtless had a dream once—childhood is about dreaming a life. But those dreams disappear, and the question is how can you find some new vision for the making or remaking of your life?

We all choose, knowingly or not, between two life strategies. You can let your life happen to you. Or you can be a dreamer, and make your life happen for you.

"Ah," you say, "too much has happened. Too many poor choices, too early made. Too many constraints and limitations restrict my freedom. All I can do now is wait and see." But remember, you have the freedom, the opportunity, this place of learning presents. You are here. This is a field of dreams. And just this opportunity, just this freedom to study, can be enough material with which to rewrite the script for your life and make for yourself a dramatic new story. For dreams give energy and vitality to our lives. Passion to live and to become flows from visions and dreams. In the birthplace of Helen Keller and W. C. Handy, how can you fail to know that limitations are there to be overcome? Sail onto life's great river—which the Tennessee symbolizes—with some grand destination and purpose in your heart.

You must start with purpose, not just to get a degree, but

to find for yourself and your life empowerment. There is deep meaning in the expression "alma mater." UNA is offering you a new life. But you must seize it. College is your best, and perhaps last, chance to begin anew. As Tennyson's Ulysses said, "'Tis not too late to seek a newer world."

I want to offer some concrete proposals for things to do if you want to become educated here. All these suggestions are calculated to start the process of placing you outside your safety zones. By now, through school and in life, you have set some level of expectation for yourself. You will never exceed that level—be it an ambition, in career, in academic performance—until you gain a new vision for what you might be and might do. It all starts with a dream.

First, go watch football practice. Any sport will do, but I know the Lions have a long tradition of excellence. Watch how committed the players and coaches are, the effort they make. Watch how hard they work to improve. Watch how they support each other in pursuit of a common goal.

I have come to regard student athletes as one of any school's most prized assets. These young men and women are not victims of the passivity which afflicts this age. They have come to love something—a game, but still something—with such passion that they understand the sacrifice, discipline, and commitment required to excel. What universities have not done well enough in the past is to help young athletes attach that passion to the other callings of their lives. When young people achieve that transfer, that passion, the lives that result are often spectacular. The passion to excel is rare. Athletes have it. Take a look.

I visited at our Homecoming this past weekend with Steve Brown, a football graduate of Wake Forest University and now a world-class hurdler. He missed the Olympic team last time by mere tenths of a second. He has committed himself to making the Olympics next time, and his life is organized singularly toward that pursuit. His life is a testament to dedication, commitment, and sacrifice. He is a dreamer. His dream has given him greatness. And that is and will remain true whether he ever makes the Olympic team or not.

When you watch football practice, ask yourself what you care about deeply enough to summon that kind of effort? Every time I watch our student athletes practice or perform, I regard them as living lessons in the passion to excel.

Whether you have done so in the past or not, and whether you are artsy or not, you need to spend time at UNA in the company of artists, musicians, poets, and performers. Imagination is the source of dreams. In school, we spend too much time teaching and telling what is and is not and making you memorize it. The imaginative domain concerns not what is, but what might be because of your creative engagement.

Emily Dickinson said, "I dwell in possibility/A fairer house than prose—/More numerous of windows/Superior for doors."

There are more windows and doors in your world of possibility than you imagine. Is there something you have always wanted to try? Photography? Creative writing? Piano lessons? Courses in these areas, especially if they are outside your safety zone, can be transforming. If you have always had a notion to try something—be in a play or practice Zen meditation—seize the day.

There is one other essential undertaking: choose at least one of the world's great creative works of art and make it your own. More than one is better, of course, but one is essential. I do not mean that you should merely study this work in a course. I mean that you appropriate it into your consciousness to a degree that you comprehend greatness. Choose one of Shakespeare's plays, one great painter, a Beethoven symphony, a Russian novel, or by this river, *The Adventures of Huckleberry Finn*. You must commit to this work. Depth, familiarity, and repetition are required. It is infinitely better to listen to Beethoven's Ninth Symphony nine times than hear all nine once. I propose here the work of a lifetime, but now you must start a dialog with something that has limitless capacity to teach you.

A significant part of the young lives of my sister and myself was our father's requirement that we engage in the art of public speech. At the earliest age at which speaking contests and debates became available, we were, however reluctantly, entered. One part of those contests was oral interpretation in which contestants were required to recite some poem from memory. I early came upon the poems of Robert Frost this way. Thus, I have lived with Frost virtually all my life. I have audited classes in his work, and there is always a book of his poems near at hand. Never a day or week goes by in which some aspect of some one of his poems is not present to my mind. I sometimes think that I have learned as much from Frost as from all the volumes of philosophy I have ever read. His is a work of greatness. I know it intimately, and Frost's poetry contributed immeasurable value to my life and to my education. Make some work of greatness part of the equipment of your own imagination. It will contribute greatness to you.

The arts have always been humankind's most compelling form of self-expression. In all its forms, the arts are the stuff of daily life—words, pictures, stories, sounds, movements—rendered by the imagination into forms that are capable not merely of entertaining us but of transforming us. Engaging your imagination opens you to visions and dreams.

I perhaps should have said first that you should form—intentionally, purposefully—personal relationships with members of this faculty. The education that is transforming is always personal. In dialogue, faculty members can help you recognize things about yourself in relationship to learning that you cannot possibly understand yourself. In this sense, teachers, whatever the field, are experts in the detection and development of human potential. Transformational teaching is always less about cognitive learning than human discovery. Students, in the hands of faculty mentors, come to a new understanding of themselves in relation to learning, a relationship that transforms the subject matter and the student. Every teacher values these prized relationships with students more than any other aspect of the profession. Seek these mentors.

When I ask, as I often do, about the education of wise men and women, the story is always of a small number of teachers, sometimes just one, who pointed this person's way to the path to Socratic self-understanding.

I was an undergraduate at Birmingham Southern during the turbulent first days of Dr. King's civil rights revolution. I shall never forget those souls in the Philosophy and Religion Department who held our hands and guided our hearts toward new moral and spiritual understandings. These guides and mentors are here for you, but you must evidence your interest in being more than a taker of courses. Engagement with faculty members inevitably exacts a price in your commitment. These relationships are central to education here and to your life.

All that I have said so far, if you should decide to be educated here rather than go to school, you can do right here using just the freedom that your presence on campus provides. Even if you live and work off campus, how you invest your hours here is the only choice I am challenging you to make. My next suggestion costs money, but it may well be the best money you ever spend: travel to a foreign land for study. If you cannot go for study, then at least go. If there is a place in your dreams that you have imagined—Rome, London, Paris, wherever—go there. If you must borrow the money, go. If what you can manage is a mission trip with your church, go.

Doors to foreign study can be opened here in language and culture courses. But you must go at whatever sacrifice. When we survey the experiences of our graduating seniors at Wake Forest, the transforming influence of foreign study is always evident. Especially now, with the coming global economy, the importance of foreign study cannot be overstated.

My wife will tell you that a year in France was more important to her intellectually than everything else she did in school. That testimony is the uniform and universal report of those who live and study abroad. You never see yourself and your home country so well, or so clearly, as when you are looking from afar. Being taken out of all that is known and familiar—away from all your safety zones—can contribute remarkably to your re-creation. The person who leaves for foreign study is seldom the same person who returns.

How do I know that this act of creation and recreation at a university can happen? Why do I believe that it is available to each of you? Because I have watched young people over many years undergo this life-altering transformation. More particularly, you have been preceded on this campus by dreamers whose visions have become the ambitions that have formed their lives. In the arts, there have been Frank Fleming, Walt Aldridge, T. S. Stribling, Nick Nichols, and George Lindsey. In business, there is Wendell Wilkie Gunn, David Kennedy, Jim Bennett, Weston Smith, and hosts of others. There have been scientists, scholars, athletes, builders, politicians, and soldiers—dreamers all. They walked these halls. They found at UNA the tools with which to make their dreams the substance of their lives. Will you join them?

At a recent meeting of student leaders at Wake Forest, our campus chaplain recited a small homily by Shel Silverstein in his book, *A Light in the Attic*, called "Magic Carpet." It expresses my message to you on this day in which we honor dreamers and visionaries.

*You have a magic carpet*

*That will whiz you through the air, to Spain or*

*Maine or Africa*

*If you just tell it where.*

*So will you let it take you*

*Where you've never been before,*

*Or will you buy some drapes to match*

*And use it on your floor?*

Here is the choice you are making or may have already made. Will you let life happen to you? In that case, you have put your magic carpet on the floor. All you need to do is to hang the drapes. Will you make life happen for you? If so, your education, your carpet, can take you from UNA on miraculous journeys—whizzing through the air. Do not miss this ride. It is the ride of your life.

———————

FALL CONVOCATION, UNIVERSITY OF NORTH ALABAMA, OCTOBER 7, 1998

# A Christmas Reflection

I have been insufficiently careful about speaking engagements that I have accepted over the last several months. Last June, I found myself before the North Carolina Bar Association speaking as a non-lawyer to an assembly of lawyers on the role of law in contemporary American life. While my speech came out well enough, it was not given without a great deal of effort and anxiety.

Indeed, I found myself on that occasion experiencing stage fright, something I have not been subject to in a long time, and a condition that would be incapacitating in my line of work. But here I am again, following in the wake of Ed Wilson and a whole train of our most eloquent and thoughtful religious leaders, to say something about Christmas and the Christmas season. Since we are all in varying ways Christmas celebrants, there may be little I can add to what your understanding has become over the seasons.

A friend who has heard my Christmas complaining remarked that I could do my Scrooge imitation. Laura will tell you that I am not a fan of much that happens about Christmas. My reasons involve all the usual suspects. We eat, drink, celebrate, and spend too much. Christmas comes too soon and lasts too long. When the Thanksgiving turkey is still warm, Christmas is upon us. You may have seen the recent *New Yorker* cover—the Halloween witch is just leaving, the Thanksgiving turkey is on stage, and Santa is already coming. The season turns us toward excess of every sort—a kind of gluttony of body and spirit.

But, most of all, I fear and feel the weight of the emotional anticipation that surrounds Christmas. No holiday so freighted with expectations can possibly fail to disappoint. No celebration promising love, joy, peace, and goodwill among men could avoid leaving us unsatisfied at best or with the holiday blues at worst. When the presents, the real and the emotional ones, have all been opened, our outcomes seldom match our expectations.

Most of us—I certainly do—have painful as well as joyful memories of the season. It is not the commercialization that I object to so much. Commercialization would not be possible without this antecedent and potent set of expectations that Christmas generates in us, which shrewd merchandisers know how to exploit. Indeed, the whole excess of Christmas says something about the nature of the human desires that attach to this season and its celebration. Christmas picks us up and carries us in its emotional train.

So, the reservations I express and genuinely feel about Christmas are not able to restrain my own sense of participation in the seasonal celebration. I am a hostage to the music of Christmas. I love the music this season has inspired. Having been a chorister, the choral music in particular provokes a sense of the holy in me that nothing else does. One of the most glorious hymns:

*Lo! How a rose e're blooming*
*From tender stem hath sprung.*
*Of Jesse's lineage coming*
*As men of old hath sung.*
*It came a floweret bright,*
*Amid the cold of winter,*
*E're half spent was the night.*

A spiritual that I particularly cherish:

*Sweet Little Jesus Boy,*
*They made You be born in a manger.*
*Sweet little Holy child,*
*Didn't know who You were.*
*Didn't know You'd come to save us, Lord,*
*To take our sins away.*
*Our eyes were blind,*
*We couldn't see.*
*We didn't know who You were.*

These words lack the power of music, but if you can hear these melodies in your head, you know the agonizing beauty with which this music expresses the hopes and fears that—in all the years—are met in the story of the little town of Bethlehem.

Because I am by training and by instinct a philosopher, I hope you will permit me some reflections on Christmas as my gift of words of the season to you. I invite you to reflect with me since I lack the gifts that would enable me to entertain or inspire.

From a strictly theological point of view, the significance of Christmas is exceeded by our celebration. Easter is the central event of the Christian calendar. In what the theologians call "salvation history," it is not how the sacred pageant begins but how it ends that matters most to the Christian story. Yet, Easter bears none of the emotional weight of the Christmas story. Easter is a more specifically theological celebration. Christmas is a season that touches our deepest and most essentially human emotions. Easter is a cause for celebration. Christmas provokes yearnings and feelings too deep for words.

The whole aura of Christmas is emotionally laden. Why is this so? What is it about the Christmas season that provokes these responses to which are given liturgical, public, and social expression, all of which in turn reinforce and reaffirm these fundamental emotional realties?

These instinctive feelings are, in my opinion, the reality that forms the root of all religions. No fact about humankind, everywhere and always, is more universal than religious belief. We are simply believing creatures. Such divine belief, it seems to me, grows from the fundamental emotional realities with which we all live. There are, of course, nonbelievers, but such nonbelief is generally an achievement—the outcome of some consciously adopted ideology. The natural state of humankind is to relate our own lives to transcendence, even when our believing is inarticulate and unreasoned.

William James spoke of "the will to believe" in God as a will that we express despite the pain and disappointment of our personal lives and the violent history of the race. Despite war, famine, pestilence, and death, we still cry out "Immanuel—God with us." Evidence of the rational cause-and-effect sort is not the source of our believing. It comes from something more profound than mere evidence.

What are these instinctive believing emotions? How are they formed and how do they relate to Christmas? They are, first and foremost, the love and dependency of family. Humans are social animals. We cannot survive alone, and the family is our basic and fundamental emotional reality. The family unit is the defining human social experience. Who and what we are as human beings derives from our experience in families. A psychiatrist friend once told me that we enact our experience in our family in every social group to which we ever belong.

Father Samuel Weber is a Dominican monk. When the Wake Forest Divinity School opens next fall, he will be our professor of spiritual formation. It will be his responsibility to lead our students in their understanding of the internal life of prayer and spirituality.

I had an extraordinary interview with him prior to his

appointment. The Dominicans are renowned, of course, for their spiritual disciplines, matters about which the Protestant tradition is generally silent. I wanted to know, of course, what kinds of gifts these were, and how could they be taught? I opened the interview by asking him whether spiritual gifts were of the sort that anyone could acquire them or if they were like musical talents, given to some and not to others. History would seem to suggest that spiritual leaders are few and particularly gifted by God. Father Weber said something that placed spirituality in the realm of the experience of each of us. When I asked Father Weber how teaching and learning of spiritual gifts was possible, he replied that the place to begin is in those spaces in our lives wherein we learn to give and receive love.

Those places are, first and foremost, our families. The family is the primitive unit within which all our earliest and most fundamental emotional connectedness is formed. In families we learn to give and receive love, lessons we take with us from childhood as we form our own families. If Father Weber is correct, in families we are at once learning something about love divine as well as human love.

This connects this source of spirituality to Christmas. The Christmas story is a story of a family, a holy family. Because of this connection to those emotions that create and sustain human life, all families are holy. That ideal of divine love, so Father Weber said, is presented to us in the love of our families. The Christmas season celebrates the holiness of primitive familial bonds and calls forth these profound and sustaining emotions.

The Christmas memories that matter most are the memories of childhood and children. We remember our parents, grandparents, and those whose gifts to us gave us the capacity to learn of love. Christmas excites and exalts these emotions, and the remembrance of them is full of awe. Christmas celebrates family, and all those emotions created in families. In Father Weber's view, this is holy ground.

But the Christmas saga is not simply a testimony to the power of family in the formation of our deepest emotions. It is the story of a baby's birth within a family. Babies—not just our own flesh and blood, but all babies—arouse our deepest and most nurturing and caring instincts. Babies are needy and helpless, and they remain so for a long period of time. Again, this is a fundamental social fact of humans. Human children must receive constant nurture that they cannot request or deserve, but which is called forth by the deepest caring instincts of the adult community. Were that not so, humans would never have survived.

This spontaneous affection for infants is everywhere evident. Sean and Eileen Fennelly, a Wake Forest law school couple who live in the garage apartment of the President's House, have become members of our extended family. Recently, they presented our household with Mary Katherine. She was the first birth under our roof that Laura and I have experienced in many years. We have been reminded powerfully of what a precious gift each new baby is. The tender overwhelming love she spontaneously provokes in us is a kind of miracle. Mary Katherine's doings—her first smiles—dominate our conversations. She is not literally our relative, but she has captured our hearts utterly.

She had only to be born, and she bestows a gift of love on all of us. Do you hear again Father Weber's lesson?

So, in the Christmas story, the holy child of Bethlehem, born in a manger, provokes our tender affection not initially because he was holy, but because he was a human child. In that sense, the angels sing at the birth of each child—each child being a new promise; something mysterious and holy; something helpless and needy but summoning our every caring instinct. Thus does Christmas touch us where we are most vulnerable to love—in the birth of a baby, a love no one can resist.

Wordsworth said, "The child is the father of the man." In that sense, we never outgrow those primitive dependencies and attachments of the child. In the face of fate and all of life's uncertainties, like the baby whose cries are fervent pleas for help, our prayers go forth reflecting our own need and dependency to a transcendent parent who alone can minister to our needs. Humankind's deep secret is that we are all dependent and helpless in the face of the universe of chance.

While we know that all language about God is metaphorical or analogical, it is no surprise that the language of faith is the language of family—the child seeking the protection, the caring intervention, of the parent. Thus, Jesus taught us to pray, "Our Father, who art in heaven." We can understand, too, those traditions that offer us feminine powers, saints, and angels, to whom we can make petition. In a room when we are talking, Mary Katherine's eyes are drawn to female voices.

This is the power of Christmas: that it celebrates these fundamental passions by which we are created, brought into the world, and sustained in our lives. Christmas is about those basic human emotional realities in which we learn to give and receive that love, which, Father Weber believes, opens us to that love all loves excelling.

So, this is why the Christmas season is filled with such passion and intensity. Its excess is that it arises from our most fundamental experiences and needs as humans. But more, Christmas calls forth an equally passionate need that, for this season, we transform these caring instincts into the reality of our experience. Christmas causes us to believe that we can love others as we love ourselves—at least for a season. As Matthew tells us, the meek can inherit the earth. The poor in spirit can possess the kingdom. Those that mourn can be comforted. The merciful can obtain mercy.

The blessing of a holy child and the choruses of angels evoke our deepest dream—that peace rather than war should govern among ns. The dream of peace on Earth, goodwill to men, so strong, so historically futile, burns at Christmas. Christmas causes us to bless the world with works of love.

Christmas summons our active goodwill, growing from our passionate and instinctive attachments, to make of the world a place where every family will sit down in unity at a full table, where presents will bring joy to every child. At least for a day or a season, we can hear and heed those impossible requirements of love: "Love your enemies, bless them that curse you, do good to them that hate you, and pray for them which despitefully use you and persecute you," as Matthew puts it.

Let me summarize by citing the marvelous lines of Robert Frost's "The Pasture." This is not a Christmas poem, exactly. But it is a child's poem and expresses what I find central to this season of the year. The poem points toward those spiritual realities that account for the deep emotional pull of the Christmas season:

> *I'm going out to clean the pasture spring; I'll*
>
> *only stop to rake the leaves away*
>
> *(And wait to watch the water clear, I may);*
>
> *I shan't be gone long—You come too.*
>
> *I'm going out to fetch the little calf*
>
> *That's standing by the mother.*
>
> *It's so young It totters when she licks*
>
> *it with her tongue.*
>
> *I shan't be gone long—You come too.*

Why is this a lesson for today? First, the poem is an invitation: "You come too." Since the invitation is to engage in the works of love, it becomes an invitation to a pilgrimage. The pilgrimage is to do the works of conservation and nurture—to clean the pasture spring, preserving the water, the symbol of life, and to fetch the young calf, so young and vulnerable that its legs are not yet for walking. The water and the calf must be given our protective love. The pilgrimage is real, and the works of love are saving. Yet, the journey is brief: "I shan't be gone long."

Christmas is this way. The season summons us all to participate in a holy pilgrimage. We are all called, as were the shepherds and wise men of old, to go to our respective Bethlehems—"You come too"—and there to do the work of conservation and care. We give alms to the poor. The Salvation Army bells cause us to stop and give. We reach out to those we love. We want each child to have at least one joyous day. We give thanks with gifts to those who serve with us each day. Christmas provokes this powerful, arresting need to extend this care everywhere to make the promises of the season real. We yearn to take the Christmas story from the gospel and make it true in Winston-Salem.

But we do not succeed in remaking the world at Christmas. We are not gone long. The lights and decorations come down. Life reasserts itself. The dreams of peace, goodwill among men, become again hopes and not imperatives.

But we are better for the journey and the world is better for our labor. Christmas brings its own clearing of the springs of our lives and opportunities to rescue those who are vulnerable and exposed. Thus, the baby born, as the shepherds and the wise men witnessed, begins a journey of good tidings of great joy that shall be to all people.

But the Kingdom of God is not of this world, and no seasonal pilgrimage—no labor of human hands—can transform the messianic hope of Israel into the kingdom on this world.

Christmas beckons in words, in songs, in the gatherings of family and friends, and in ancient rituals. We shall not fail to come as summoned. Though we shall not be gone long, we must arise and go to our respective Bethlehems. The work of love is there to do.

May a star from the east guide your pilgrimage this season and direct the labor of your hands as you do holy work in the pastures of your Christmas and as you return soon to the land of your living and your work to plan your resolutions for the year to come.

———————————

CHRISTMAS MEETING, THE ROTARY CLUB OF WINSTON-SALEM, DECEMBER 15, 1998

# Christmas Joy and Sorrow

Despite the fact that this holiday season celebrates joy, good cheer, peace and happiness—or more likely because this time of year exalts these glad emotions—Christmas always brings an inevitable undercurrent of melancholy and sadness. Most of us, in one way or another, know what is meant by "the holiday blues."

Christmas is, first of all, a season of memory, and Christmas memories are bittersweet at best. Those memories are of the disappointments and excitements of the season as well as the remembrance of our own lost childhoods. Most poignantly, the memories are of those who loved us when we were children and whose absence is most keenly felt at Christmas. The places, the people, and the times that gave Christmas its emotional character are lost to us. For many of us, Christmas comes with joy and sorrow in almost equal portions.

So, on this happy holiday occasion, it is not inappropriate, I trust, that I offer reflections about grief and grieving. Grief is, of course, inherent in the experience of love. The recognition of the fragile nature of love gives the intensity of love its underlying uncertainty. Grief is as essential and inevitable an emotion as love itself. Ultimately, grief is the tribute we pay to love when love is lost. There is no human love, no great love, that does not offer the risk of loss and grief.

We have special reason this year to think of grief and grieving at Christmas. The national tragedy of September 11 remains fresh and near. The nation has been grieving ever since, not alone for those lost and the pain of their families. We are also in grief for the end of the security and safety that "Fortress America" has always represented. Our schools, offices, and homes are insecure as they have never been before. Our former separation from a dangerous world has been lost. The things near and dear are in jeopardy—as near as our mailboxes.

In the days following September 11, our alumni office arranged a telethon to contact Wake Forest University alumni and friends in the greater New York area. Our purpose was to ascertain their safety and well-being and to offer any assistance we might provide. We learned from those phone calls that our common national tragedy, for those dear souls near Ground Zero, had been multiplied many times over as they suffered losses of friends, business associates, parents of their children's friends, family soccer coaches, Sunday school teachers, and neighbors. One alumnus I spoke with had been to six memorial services, and he was not finished with his sad duty. His heart was broken, and in the hearing of his grief, so was mine.

The *New York Times* has been publishing a section entitled

"Portraits of Grief." These are brief life vignettes of those lost in the murderous attack of September 11. I am inevitably drawn to these portraits, despite the fact that they regularly bring me to tears and agonizing grief. The portraits remind me that what happened that awful day transcended national tragedy. There were thousands upon thousands of private and personal tragedies. Each victim was part of a wide circle of love now broken. There will be scores of families who will gather this Christmas with an empty place at their tables and in their hearts.

However painful, these portraits each day put me in touch with this extraordinary personal loss, as did those phone calls. This is a bitter, sorrowful lesson, but a lesson we are forced to learn intellectually and emotionally.

Thus, this Christmas we must consider grief and the process of grieving lest this sadness overwhelm us. We generally regard grief as a process, passing through stages aimed at a recovery, a process aimed at a restoration of our normal emotional equilibrium. But in reflecting upon the personal grief that I have known and the grief that I am now experiencing with you and with our comrades in New York, Washington, and Pennsylvania, this notion of grief as the recovery of our normal, prior state of being seems inadequate. Because grief reflects the loss of so fundamental an experience as love, there is no recovery, no returning to our previous state of normality. That former state of being—the absence of lost love—is no longer who we are.

Rather, the end of grief is a kind of rebirth, an emotional reincarnation in which we enter a new reality, a new kind of psychic equilibrium. The end of grieving is not the restoration of the normal. The end of grief is renewal, a kind of human resurrection. Given lost love, the normal must be recreated, reinvented as part of a new emotional world. Since my mother died, life has not been the same for me. I suspect you can reflect upon your own losses and understand what I mean.

Grief is not something to "get over" or "live through." It is a movement toward a new normal, aiming at a different way and place of living and being. Without my mother to consult or counsel me, I am no longer the person I was. It took me many months to realize that I was not going to "recover" from her loss.

That is why these remarks about grief and grieving find a place in the Christmas story, and why we do well to embrace the sadness as well as the joy this season offers. For the Christmas saga is, above all, a story about the end of the old and the beginning of the new. In the birth of the Christ child is symbolized the beginning of a new human reality that summons us to become new creatures. The old order is gone. A new reality begins.

We are summoned by lost love and grief to go to our respective Bethlehems—the places of beginning—and to return, no longer possessing what we have lost but reaching forward to what we can become in newness of spirit and heart. As St. Paul said, "The old order has passed away. Behold, all things are become new." That is the message of Christmas, and that is the hope of this Christmas—being transformed by the "renewal of our minds."

Thus, if we can set our hearts on the renewal and the rebirth that the holiday season promises, despite our grief and loss, or again perhaps because of our grieving, we may claim for our very own—and offer to each other—that ancient and wonderful and attainable holiday blessing: "Have A Merry, Merry Christmas."

———————————

REMARKS TO REYNOLDA HALL, CHRISTMAS CELEBRATION, DECEMBER 19, 2001

# Legal Ethics and Corporate Governance Post Enron

## - Conference Closing Remarks -

As a once-upon-a-time professor of moral theory, the topic of this conference has played a professional as well as a personal role in my own life. On the personal side, as some of you know, I grew up in a remote area of northwest Alabama, the end of Appalachia. The principles of right conduct taught in those days were simple and clear. There were established norms of the family, the church, and the state. Our duty was obedience to these norms and reverence toward the sources of normative authority.

Happiness did not consist in doing what I might have wanted but in fulfilling my duties as they were assigned by these sources of authority. It would not have occurred to my father that my personal happiness could consist of anything other than the obedience appropriate to children.

This ordered moral universe of my childhood, however, was to be overturned. The year 1954 marked the Supreme Court decision in Brown v. Board of Education. In 1955, I graduated from an all-white high school. In 1956, the bus boycott in Montgomery began. Thus, during my undergraduate years, a moral, legal, and spiritual revolution unfolded. The philosophy and religion departments were where these topics were discussed and explained, and so I gravitated there. As a sophomore, I had a classroom illumination that the person at the front of the room was being paid money to read books and talk about them, and I knew at once that higher education was the life for me!

The world as I had known it had to be remade while I was a student. It was clear to me as an undergraduate that education had, and must have, moral purpose. My undergraduate years brought revolutionary changes in my understanding of myself, my duties, and the religious tradition in which I had been nurtured. True to that sophomore epiphany, I went on to earn a PhD in moral philosophy and entered the world of university teaching.

The end of the 1960s found me on the faculty of the College of William and Mary as the cultural revolution broke over our campuses. Whether the issues were the sexual revolution and abortion or civil disobedience and the Vietnam War, I worked to make my classroom a place for moral discussion and clarification. Part of what I had come to believe as a teacher of moral philosophy was that few people had ever thought clearly and systematically about the moral life—moral beliefs being a patchwork drawn from here and there. I tried to correct that deficit in my students with all the zeal of a young teacher.

William and Mary enrolled scores of students from the Washington, D.C. area, many of whom where the children of military and diplomatic personnel. The Vietnam War was for these young people a critical and personal issue of divisive family impact. Should a child of a military family seek conscientious objector status? While such questions were deeply personal and emotional, they also offered a perfect opportunity for the growth of understanding and perspective. We often experienced together what we later learned to call "teachable moments."

Does education have a moral purpose? Of course it does. The broadening of our understanding leads to an extension of our sympathy and an enlarged affinity for the perspective of others. That was my experience as a student. It was also my experience as a teacher.

I shall always, of course, be grateful for the kindly providence that, in time, brought me to Wake Forest University. Here was a place where our creed and motto, Pro Humanitate, embodied my own faith and experience that education is for human betterment. This was my intellectual, moral home.

Nowhere at Wake Forest is this ethical tradition more firmly entrenched than in our school of law. Many of you here will remember when an interview with Dean Weathers was required for admission to our school of law. His concern was always as much for morals and motivation as intellect.

We have been discussing this weekend an ancient topic: can ethics be taught? Is it a kind of knowledge, or are moral values the outcomes of custom and habit alone? With that question Socrates launched moral reflection in the Western intellectual experience.

I came to believe as an undergraduate that the Socratic view that "virtue is knowledge" was right. There is moral knowledge. It can be taught, as everyone who has participated in the upbringing of a child knows. And, of course, many professors of law (and some professors of philosophy) can testify to the growth of moral understanding that takes place in our classrooms.

When people say that ethics cannot be taught, what they often mean is that ethical "teaching" does not guarantee ethical "conduct." Courses in ethics do not produce ethical persons. If the lesson of Genesis is to be believed, we all do destructive and evil things. The cause is often not moral ignorance; it is rather more often moral failure. We do what we know to be wrong. I know it is wrong to tell the lies I tell.

In a similar way, teaching about safety does not ensure that we act safely. We humans are easy prey to temptation of every kind. As Oscar Wilde once put it, "I can resist everything except temptation."

The world at the opening of this new millennium has a great deal more moral clutter than it did in the hills of Alabama a few decades ago. Our job as ethical teachers, a job we all perform every day, has become more difficult, exceedingly so. The causes of this clutter are many and complex. There is the decline of the stability of the family, and increased social mobility separates us from our relatives and mentors. Mobility deters the formation of stable moral relationships. The ascent of the mass media and popular culture means that children are presented with a daily dose of "moral" instruction that celebrates personal indulgence, violence, drugs, and intoxication. I sometimes think that we can scarcely overcome these dismal influences.

The growing diversity of our culture means that we must learn to respect and regard the customs and beliefs of those unlike ourselves. As a philosopher might put it, we must learn to accept "otherness" into our awareness and understanding.

While the moral universe of my childhood has been undone, I affirm that the basic moral tenants of the simple moral theory I was taught at home, at school, and at church are primarily the domain of moral knowing: do justice, love mercy, and walk humbly with God.

This general decline in the rigor and reach of personal morality, however, has had the most profound social consequences, for personal morality is the primary and critical form of social regulation. Every other sort of external regulation will present us a loss of personal autonomy. But in the decline of personal and public morality, other forms of social regulation have been of necessity expanded, primary among them being the law. The law now controls ever-expanding domains of private and public life. We often complain of this reach of the law, sometimes with just cause. Howard's *The Death of Common Sense* speaks directly to this condition, and it makes dismal reading.

However, the reach and scope of the law is a function not of the law itself but of the society we have come to be and have chosen to be. Think of the importance of antidiscrimination laws of various kinds. Consider environmental and safety regulations. Unknown a few decades ago, such laws are now basic to our personal and social values.

Thus, as the role of law and the influence of lawyers have grown, it is urgent that the values of the legal profession and legal ideals be promulgated and taught as well and as thoroughly as the skills and techniques of the profession. There will, of course, be greedy and corrupt lawyers who will pervert their training to secure ill-gotten advantages. But let us work without ceasing to do all we can to ensure that such lawyers do not wear the colors of our university and thus bring our law school and our university into disregard.

More than abstract moral precepts, the law school must always facilitate the development of personal relationships by faculty with students whereby ideals are presented not just by teaching but by the friendship that lifts the ambitions of students. The teacher is powerful when her or his influence is direct and personal. Ideals are best seen on two feet.

In considering the morality of this great profession, we must never forget that the rule of law is modern democratic civilization's singular achievement. We have only to look at places in the world lacking this achievement to understand how fundamental it is to our personal and social well-being. We dare not take this blessing for granted. The legal profession must decide how the massive new influence of the law will be directed.

We must see that graduates of the Wake Forest University School of Law serve the needs of a free people for a system of justice that advances, and does not impede, the orderly processes of our lives and of our work.

In thus adhering to the ideals of the profession, the law will be an institution deserving of our reverence, and "lawyer" will be a title of service and honor.

———————————

WAKE FOREST UNIVERSITY LAW LEADERSHIP COUNCIL
WAKE FOREST UNIVERSITY BOARD OF TRUSTEES
SUMMER LEADERSHIP CONFERENCE
THE HOMESTEAD, JULY 31 TO AUGUST 3, 2003

# Religious Heritage
# and Academic Culture
# at Wake Forest

From the period when education at Wake Forest University became an enterprise clearly distinct from evangelism—the work of the university thus being separate and not subordinate to the mission of the church—we have struggled with the question of our religious identity and responsibility. The issues arising from this question have been vexing, often controversial, and something in our common character is doubtless owed to the fact that we were often at odds with North Carolina Baptists over issues as large as academic freedom and as trivial as dancing.

The question of Wake Forest's religious identity has now

assumed an unprecedented character. We no longer have any official or formal ties to the North Carolina Baptist Convention. Last year, in response to criticism of our campus alcohol policies and the university's posture regarding the Wake Forest Baptist Church—an independent congregation that worships in our chapel—the Convention severed our remaining relationships, referring to Wake Forest as a "historically-related institution."

This means that Wake Forest must decide the significance of our religious heritage without the constraint or the requirement of any external condition or relationship. Thus, will we be a better university—academically and in the environment provided for students—if we seek to integrate this Christian heritage into our future or if we, in time, come to disregard it? That most important question is before Wake Forest now and in the years ahead.

Based upon the work of historian George Marsden and others (for example, *The Secularization of the Academy*), we can reasonably predict what, left to the prevailing norms of the academy, the answer to the question would be. In *The Soul of the American University*, Marsden documents the broad intellectual forces—scientism, objectivity, academic freedom, cultural pluralism, and others—which caused many elite universities in America of Protestant origin to repudiate the principles of their founding and of their distinguished histories. Christianity in these schools is not only "peripheral" but also "absolutely alien" to the academic enterprise. Woodrow Wilson regularly preached at mandatory chapel at Princeton. Founding documents proclaiming "the external union of knowledge and religion as set forth in the teachings and character of Jesus Christ" would have been typical in some of our best schools well into the twentieth century. Noah Porter, president of Yale, was also president of the Wellesley College board, whose founders asserted Wellesley to be "Christian in its influence, discipline, and course of instruction."

What is to be our future with respect to our own religious identity now that the question is in our hands and that of our governing board?

I want to suggest that our religious heritage is a source of strength and vitality, and that the Lilly program which we are inaugurating today provides an important opportunity to incorporate this heritage into our present work and life.

## The Pervasive Cultural Force of Religion

In *When Religion Becomes Evil*, Charles Kimball remarks that religion "is arguably the most powerful and pervasive force on earth." The ebb and flow of history and the rise and fall of cultures and civilizations demonstrate the truth of his claim in an historical sense. In contemporary terms as well, religion is definitive for culture, and provides the conceptual framework by which human beings around the world interpret their lives and their experience, and the terms by which humans ask and answer basic existential questions of meaning and destiny. In a comprehensive sense, therefore, religion is both the metaphysics and the moral foundation of humanity. The events of 9/11 brought matters of religious culture to the world's attention in a way not soon to be forgotten.

This almost universal influence of religion is not merely a historical or sociological matter. It has profound implications for the intellectual architecture, the conceptual systems, upon which all knowledge—and thus all teaching and learning—rests. Because of religion's reach across history and culture, and the centrality of religion to the psychology of human understanding, it could be argued that religion is the discipline most basic to liberal education.

On the face of it, therefore, it would not seem wise for institutions that value liberal education—and not just specialized knowledge—to follow the path which Marsden's work would suggest for an institution with a history and foundation like ours. Unless we understand religion—and approach it as religion, as lived and practiced—we shall understand neither our own worldview nor, just as urgently, the worldviews of others. Kimball's book, *When Religion Becomes Evil*, is a forceful case in point.

Religions make claims about the world—claims that are conceptually basic and fervently disputed. These disputes pose the most basic questions about epistemological limits. In our tradition, this matter has taken the form of a long and important debate about the domains of faith and reason. In the modern era, this debate is more acutely focused as a result of the intellectual stature achieved by the empirical sciences. What is at issue is not merely religious knowledge, or lack of it, but the larger claim that all knowledge is confined to the limits of empirical science.

This claim—one of the most powerful forces at work in the academy and in culture—has profound implications for teaching and learning. For what shall we say about art, literature, philosophy, or the social sciences? Do these disciplines, as well as religion, contribute to human understanding or are these subjects merely highbrow human entertainments? The claims of religion, along with those of the arts and humanities, require that we explore questions upon which much about the entire academic enterprise depends. We are a better university—a richer and more diverse educational culture—to the extent that these matters are at issue in our classrooms and residence halls.

Let me provide another local example of how matters of religion are fundamental to education and culture. Wake Forest's Michael Perry is a leading legal scholar whose work deals prominently with the role of religion in legal and political matters.

The moral foundation of democracy resides in the idea that human beings occupy a unique moral status. Regardless of individual differences, persons—merely as persons—possess natural, inalienable rights. Immanuel Kant argued that persons are ends in themselves—possessing inherent dignity and worth.

No idea has been more powerful and important to democracy than the notion of human rights, from the fight over abolition, to establishing the moral and legal basis of the Nuremberg trials, to the extension of freedoms and opportunities to minority populations in America and around the world.

Perry and others claim that the idea of human rights is an essentially religious idea, the suggestion captured in the formulation of rights which asserts that human life is sacred. In an intriguing series of arguments, developed in *The Idea of Human Rights: Four Inquiries*, Perry suggests that no secular version of the notion of human rights can be sustained. This is a striking and important conclusion. Arguments about rights, their extension and their limits, fill our policy debates, not to mention the political media. I dare say that few, if any, of the partisans to these debates recognize that their moral claims have led them to the realm of theological discourse.

## Our Story's Beginning

The Wake Forest story begins with Reverend Samuel Wait traveling through eastern North Carolina in 1827 collecting funds for Columbia College. As the result of a spooked horse and a damaged wagon, Reverend Wait was detained for a week in New Bern where he preached in the local congregations. The worshippers were impressed, and he was called to the pulpit of the New Bern Baptist Church.

Dr. Wait's concern for education and the cultivation of the ministry, however, took a new form. With the support of other leaders in the North Carolina Baptist Convention, the Wake Forest Manual Labor Institute was born, soon to become a college and, not until 1967, a university. Our subsequent history reflects an ongoing concern to be respectful of this founding religious commitment, while at the same time pursuing our developing understanding of our responsibility as an institution of higher education.

Our board of trustees was self-perpetuating from the founding of Wake Forest until the early part of the last century, when the power of election was ceded to the North Carolina Baptist Convention. In the 1970s, Wake Forest was given the right to nominate a small number of non-North Carolinians and non-Baptists to our board, reflecting the fact that we were no longer exclusively a North Carolina institution—though these nominees were actually elected by the Convention and there remained a religious qualification for service.

In time, the Convention came to exercise virtual veto power over the appointments of non–North Carolina Baptists by insisting on the right to make an independent and religious judgment of their fitness to be elected after our trustees had nominated them.

In the 1980s, the trustees, responding to increased tension over the election process, were able to reach an arrangement whereby the board again became self-perpetuating, ending the roughly six decades of control by the Convention. In return, Wake Forest surrendered all claims of support by the Baptist Convention. That agreement was described as "fraternal and voluntary," and Wake Forest retained associate membership on various educational councils and was listed as a North Carolina Baptist institution until the changes of last year. Today, our governing board no longer asserts any geographical or religious requirements for membership.

Throughout this long and often controversial series of developments, our mission statements have affirmed the importance of our Baptist heritage and the centrality of our religious identity to our academic life and work. Indeed, it was after our formal separation from the Convention that the trustees established the Divinity School. The School affirms that we should provide leadership for the church as we do for the other great professions and vocations, thus making our relationship to our religious heritage a part of our academic mission. We serve the church as we serve law, education, medicine, business, and the other avenues of public service.

In ways we did not altogether anticipate, the Divinity School has already forged important links with the Winston-Salem community, facilitating religious dialogue and service through internships and mentors. Its ecumenical efforts have extended or strengthened our connections with Presbyterians, United Methodists, Moravians, Roman Catholics, Lutherans, Quakers, Pentecostals, and members of the Jewish community. The Divinity School will facilitate summer programs funded by Lilly and offer high school students an opportunity for service learning and exploration of ministerial vocation.

## Pressures of Public Notice

For the present and for the foreseeable future, I do not believe that our trustees will permit the repudiation or erosion of our religious heritage. But the fact is that for as long as we were a small regional institution, the academic world little cared what Wake Forest did. Now that we are page 1 in the *U.S. News* and other rankings, the forces of academic conformity and uniformity are much more in evidence. There is a widely shared notion that academic excellence has a univocal meaning defined often by those very institutions Marsden's history describes.

Part of our board's outlook is simply the debt which we owe the past. Wake Forest would not exist, nor would it have survived the perils of an often-turbulent history, especially the Civil War, without the resolve and commitment of North Carolina Baptists. Many of the benefactions we received—such as the Bostwick gift from a Standard Oil Co. founder that created our modern endowment—were given because we were a Baptist school serving the needs of a Baptist people in a then remote location. Despite Wake Forest's formal separation from the church, that history with its contributions and inherent obligations does not disappear. Who and what we are is inevitably a function of who and what we have been.

But there are other elements of our corporate personality that owe much to the Baptist tradition. Our history of contention with the church, sometimes friendly and sometimes fierce, was itself a reflection of the very Baptist idea of freedom, and freedom has been a central tenet at Wake Forest. Perhaps few of us now know that Wake Forest was awarded the Alexander Meiklejohn Freedom Award for the defense of academic freedom from the American Association of University Professors in 1978 because of the stand Wake Forest took against the church's opposition to federal involvement in higher education.

I believe there is a consensus on our board that just as Brandeis affirms its Jewish and Notre Dame its Catholic identity, Wake Forest should not deny its heritage in the Christian and Baptist communions. The corporate entity that is Wake Forest is as tangible a reality as those of us who are individual agents in the drama that is its life across the generations. Wake Forest—the collective reality—has a particular religious identity.

I hasten to add that this religious posture is compatible with our respect for religious pluralism and the desire, even the necessity, that we hear and heed different and dissenting voices.

At one level, this is because we are devoted to learning from others the alternative ways in which transcendence has been construed. But in purely religious terms, the Baptist insistence that there is no prescribed orthodox code of belief—no creed—means that we must all posit the propositions of faith with humility and the recognition that we cannot contain divine truth in human formulations. Each person being a priest means that no one person can affirm his or her own faith formula as divinely ordained. We live and we walk by faith.

This is the Baptist outlook—radical and antinomian as it is—and not some version prescribed by the ideas of political correctness and diversity. In fact, Wake Forest lived this creed. When the Jewish Artom family fled Italian fascism, they came to old Wake Forest where they were so loved that when Professor Artom became an internationally recognized scientist and might have served at any number of more prestigious medical centers, he would never leave the place that gave his family a home when they had none. The Artoms arrived by train in old Wake Forest speaking no English. Bianca Artom loved to tell that her introduction to America was to be given a milkshake and taken to a basketball game! Our academic center in Venice, Casa Artom, honors this Jewish legacy at Wake Forest. Baptist freedom at Wake Forest embraced the Jewish Artoms, not with tolerance, but with love.

Thus, contrary to what contemporary stereotypes suggest, being a Baptist school did not mean that Wake Forest was closed or rigid. The famous advocacy of William Louis Poteat for the teaching of evolution meant that North Carolina—

alone of the Southern states—did not adopt an anti-evolution statute. So signal was his achievement that he was given honorary degrees by Chapel Hill and Duke! Dr. Poteat drew deep from the well of the Baptist tradition in his insistence upon individual freedom and responsibility. Freedom of religion has a strong parallel in the venerated tradition of academic freedom on this campus.

Though all America has much to be ashamed of in the matter of race relations, Wake Forest was the first private Southern university to integrate. When the Communist scare of the 1950's brought a speaker ban to the public universities of this state, Wake Forest brought a perennial Communist political candidate to speak on our campus. We opened our forums to Norman Thomas, the socialist, as well as George Lincoln Rockwell, head of the American Nazi party. Reflecting on this heritage, I fear we may now be less free in our willingness to hear all positions on all topics than we were when those freedom-worshipping Baptists ruled these halls.

In honoring this religious heritage and in claiming this part of our corporate personality, Wake Forest acknowledges an element of our past which directed us at critical moments to choose freedom—academic freedom, freedom of expression, and freedom of religion—with all the controversy that freedom engenders. This is not a history to be overcome or set aside. This is a history to be prized and nurtured.

## Liberal Education and Religious Belief

If this assessment of the centrality of religion to liberal education and the significance of our own heritage be granted, the importance of the religious environment extends as well to campus life and culture. The ideal of liberal education concerns human wholeness and directs reflection toward questions of meaning and destiny. Most of our students arrive with explicitly religious commitments and concerns, and we can hardly provide for their intellectual and moral maturity without providing an atmosphere hospitable to religious deliberation and practice.

An educational institution is not a church, but a university is a place where beliefs, perhaps especially religious commitments, are examined and considered in the process of developing a mature religious and intellectual outlook. Perhaps no feature of the Wake Forest experience has been so persistently and appreciatively reported to me by alumni over the years than accounts of a youthful religious faith and practice being transformed here into a sustaining and mature religious life.

Much of this religious activity, of course, belongs in the domain of practice presided over by our chaplains and campus ministers. But much religious development has a more explicitly academic foundation, and not just in religion courses. An academic program where religious questions and issues are subjected to historic and systematic study is calculated to inform and, at times, to reform faith, as well as to extend understanding of ourselves and others.

Much has changed on the nation's campuses since the repudiation of *in loco parentis* in the late 1960s and 1970s. As a young professor in the late 1960s, I regularly chaperoned student parties on weekends. They pretended, at least, that they were glad to see me! Campus social life, student organizations, personal advising, and mentoring were, I think it is fair to say, matters which the faculty regarded as part of our academic responsibility.

The narrower definition of the academic program resulting from the "cultural revolution"—to substantially exclude student life and culture—has tended to separate and isolate the campus experience of students from engagement with faculty. So we worry, as we perennially do, about the intellectual atmosphere on campus beyond the classroom and the social lives of our students left to their own devices. That worry comes, in part, from changes in how academicians now define their professional responsibilities.

Parenthetically, I should add that growing concern about alcohol and substance abuse on America's campuses is prompting a reexamination of the wisdom of this departure from in loco parentis. There is, of course, an immediate and obvious connection between the environment in which students study and learn and the environment in which they live and play.

To the extent that we integrate living and learning—I believe this to be the lesson of the remarkable outcomes of our foreign study houses—we strengthen both the academic program and the social experience of our students. Much the same can be said for many of our service learning trips. Many students experience on these pilgrimages of study and service a moral and intellectual transformation.

Immanuel Kant said that the overriding questions of human life are the existence of God, the freedom of the will, and the immortality of the soul. No one can navigate life's journey without serious consideration of questions of purpose and destiny. Wake Forest should always be a place where these topics are reflected in how we study, how we live, and how we worship.

## Building on Heritage

This background will explain the importance of this occasion and why we are so pleased and honored to have received this grant from the Lilly Endowment under its "Programs for the Theological Exploration of Vocation." The resources provided by this grant offer us many ways to build upon the best of our heritage. In the area of institutional identity, it affords us a structured way to engage in sustained conversations within and among the many constituent parts of our community: faculty, staff, students, alumni, trustees, parents, and friends of Wake Forest University.

I hope that each of you here tonight—and many, many more who are not with us—will seize the opportunity to engage this process of discussion over the next five years. You will hear more in coming weeks and months as, together, we endeavor to nurture and shape our institutional identity in the twenty-first century, a course that both honors and builds upon the values that have distinguished Wake Forest and, at the same time, fully embraces the rich diversity, pluralism, and interdependence that characterize our community, nation, and world.

I want to thank all those responsible for the planning and preparation of this proposal and congratulate Betsy Taylor, who will direct the Pro Humanitate Center that was created under the grant. The Pro Humanitate Center, honoring the Wake Forest motto, implies that we will be permitted to consider the meaning of our religious heritage, to have a broad discussion on the relationship of vocation to career, and to continue our efforts to integrate the ideal of service into the Wake Forest experience.

As our students are in the process both of the formation of mature values and the establishment of their professional aspirations, it is essential that we provide avenues to consider vocation as the intersection of work and meaning. As Robert Frost said at the conclusion of "Two Tramps in Mud Time":

*My object in living is to unite*
*My avocation and my vocation*
*As my two eyes make one in sight. Only where*
*love and need are one,*
*And the work is play for mortal stakes, Is the*
*deed ever really done*
*For Heaven and the future's sake.*

The Pro Humanitate Center should assist and support our community in seeking that union of avocation and vocation, love and need, so that the work we undertake here will be for heaven and for the future.

# Conclusion

Finally, let me tell you a Wake Forest story. Last September, in the aftermath of 9/11, filled as all Americans were with grief and a sense of helplessness, our alumni office decided that we should telephone our alumni and friends living in the affected areas to ascertain their safety and to extend our concern.

All of us who made these calls will never forget those moving and often disturbing conversations. One alumnus to whom I spoke had been to five funerals in one week and did not even know how many more friends for whom he had yet to mourn.

Those phone calls said much about that agonizing moment for Americans as well as the personal experiences of those to whom we spoke. But the calls also said something about Wake Forest, about the remarkable attachment members of this community feel toward each other and toward the school.

As this sad anniversary approached this year, those same thoughtful souls in Alumni Affairs decided that we should send a short letter of concern marking the day. Let me confess that I was hesitant about this suggestion, thinking perhaps a letter too small a gesture to acknowledge such a burden of memory. I could not have been more mistaken. Again, the numerous responses to the letter were gratifying and reassuring. People were glad that we remembered, and that we were marking the day on campus with solemn ceremony.

One young alumnus, in reply to my letter, shared his harrowing 9/11 experience. He was in a building facing the World Trade Center, evacuated to safety on foot through the ordeal which left him, by his own account, an "emotional mess."

His recovery was made possible, he said, by strong community support: "This community is made up mostly of Wake Forest graduates. It is made up of Wake Forest graduates because of the sense of community that Wake Forest breeds."

Finally, he described for me his concluding reflection from this life-altering experience:

"I intended this email to be a short response to express my gratitude, but it seems it took a longer form. This seems to be a theme of September 11—that plans are ever-changing, and that life never ends up the way we thought it would. This, in essence, is why building a foundation for response is so vital. My foundation was built at Wake Forest."

May we always be a place that nurtures the building of secure foundations for the living of these days.

───────────────

LILLY ENDOWMENT, INC. PROGRAMS FOR THE THEOLOGICAL EXPLORATION OF VOCATION. ADDRESS TO THE FACULTY, SEPTEMBER 24, 2002

# Schools and American Cultural Conflict

P rivate education is a paradoxical enterprise. You and I charge a great deal of money for a credential that is provided free or at a dramatically less cost in all our neighborhoods. Private higher education, in particular, is in dramatic decline. In the 1960s roughly half of all the students in American higher education were in private colleges, a number that by the late 1990s had shrunk to roughly fifteen percent of college enrollments. This change is largely a reflection, of course, of the huge growth of public institutions, especially junior colleges. That enrollment decline would seem to predict a terrible outlook, and for some private colleges the future is uncertain. On the other hand, the paradigms of excellence in American higher education are the great private institutions. The best private colleges are flourishing, and the future could hardly be brighter.

My first task is to thank you. Those of you in the independent school sector establish in the public mind the notion that in education, as in a great many other things, you get what you pay for. Value in education is in part a function of price. You have established this notion so firmly in the K-12 sector that it secures the constituency for private universities like Wake Forest University, which many of your graduates attend. In independent schools and colleges, we are fellow travelers in a common enterprise.

I want to reflect with you about issues affecting education in general and private education in particular. Though I will use higher education as my better known and more familiar illustration, these issues are common to our calling and to all our schools.

Having been in office for a long time, I am sometimes asked about the major changes that I have observed in administration during my tenure. My answer is the growing requirement in schools for institutional effectiveness in a financial, legal, organizational, and administrative sense. In the golden age, not many years ago, schools were universally held to be places where good things were being done for young people. We were scarcely held accountable to the public. We were given resources and permitted to direct them as our best judgment dictated, with minimal oversight or accountability.

Schools now face the entire burden of federal, state, and local regulation, not to mention the academic oversight we receive from accreditors and educational agencies. The consequences of this regulatory burden for academic leadership are profound.

Wake Forest now has a legal staff larger than the entire bar in the small Alabama town where I grew up! We have a university-wide compliance office whose responsibility is to monitor changes in the regulatory environment and to see that we are prepared to enforce regulations of every sort across our schools and departments. The office carries out systematic regulatory training for our staff and faculty. Compliance is of such importance that this function reports directly to me as well as to what our trustees now call the Audit and Compliance Committee.

The impact of this changed regulatory environment on the academic culture has been dramatic. External regulatory requirements must be met with technical competence. As a result, schools have had to professionalize and expand the administration. Faculty members at Wake Forest sometimes opine, not as a compliment, that we have adopted a "corporate" style of governance. But academic judgment cannot address the specialized issues of regulation and regulators. Schools must be represented by technically competent professionals who know the rules, how they apply, and how their impact on our institutions can be managed. We must have professional, technical expertise in every area of regulatory interface. This impact is felt across the entire administration.

This changed environment is influencing executive selection in universities. When I talk to trustees or headhunters about executive searches, they are no longer exclusively interested in a candidate's intellectual experience and leadership. They are concerned whether a candidate can run the place organizationally and financially. The "executive" requirement is at least on equal footing with academic preparation.

Growing regulation is increasing the requirement of trustee oversight. This places additional burdens on our volunteer boards and can blur the distinction between the policy jurisdiction of the board and the management domain of administration. When there is an enhanced oversight requirement, boards will be reviewing larger facets of the institution's life. Good administrative and trustee communication is ever more essential for the health of our schools.

Current corporate scandals involving accounting and corporate governance will certainly compound this regulatory and reporting burden. Scandal inevitably yields regulation. Be prepared to invest more time, effort, and money on the accounting function. Standards of reporting and accountability will be changing.

As heads of schools, you must enhance your own technical competence and the organizational capacity of your schools. The Southern Association of Independent Schools, and organizations like it, can assist in this endeavor. It is no longer possible for us to be educators only. We must be competent and technically proficient managers to navigate the environment our schools now face.

## Influence of the Consumer Movement

In recent years, nothing has influenced education, certainly not higher education, more than the consumer movement. Consumerism has overtaken the educational enterprise. The most conspicuous evidence of this influence is the rating and ranking industry, which is both the cause and the effect of the consumer outlook. The *U.S. News and World Report* college guide is quite simply the "consumer report" for higher education.

Academicians rightly complain that placing schools in a rank order of merit without knowing what "good" means for which students, or in which disciplines, is a dubious undertaking. Those complaints, however, fall on deaf ears. The college issue of *U.S. News* is the largest-selling issue of any weekly news magazine year in and year out. Someone remarked that this college issue changed the position of *U.S. News* in the news magazine industry. It was this single idea—to rank schools—that brought *U.S. News* to the journalistic level of *Time* and *Newsweek*. The *U.S. News* college issue is sold out on an advertising basis for the indefinite future, and it spins off books and other materials. It is a profitable venture.

Other college guides, too, are part of a major business for the publishing industry. Next time you visit a bookstore, see how many such manuals there are. This industry reflects and enforces the consumer mentality and attitude. Academic criticism will not blunt the impact of so established a public attitude.

There are significant values in the consumer movement. It provides useful and important information to potential students. Your college counselors want their advisees to make informed decisions using reliable information about the colleges that they visit and consider, and doubtless your offices make use of these materials.

From the college side, guidebooks help get our message out. Students visiting Wake Forest now routinely know that we have a 10:1 faculty-student ratio, that we do not use teaching assistants to offer undergraduate courses, and volumes of other facts gleaned from the college guides and counselors.

*U.S. News*, of course, practices an important deceit. The ratings and rankings generally follow and reflect the reputation of a university's graduate and doctoral programs. The college issue, however, is marketed to prospective undergraduate students. What the reputational surveys reflect will seldom directly reflect the quality of the undergraduate experience.

A few years ago, some survey reported that Princeton had the fifth best law school in the country. Princeton, of course, does not have a law school! Opinion surveys are just that: opinions—good and bad, informed and otherwise.

Most importantly, the consumerist outlook distorts and misrepresents the academic enterprise. Education is an opportunity and not a commodity. It is not like a car or a dishwasher. Education cannot be "bought," but many consumers balk at this distinction. You have heard the sentence that begins "I am not paying you all this money for..." You can finish the sentence from your own experience. The general assumption is those who are paying the tuition are buying something schools must provide for their payment.

Consumerism empowers the customer rather than the provider, making the parent rather than the teacher or the school the expert in the educational transaction. I am buying this; therefore, I know what it is I want. A parent's vision for a child's education is often not the school's or even the child's vision.

A parent friend called me in dire distress to say that his child had decided to major in theatre. "What can you do about it?" my friend asked. I had the daughter come in, and, as you might expect, she had the best of reasons for doing what she, and not her father, wanted. I phoned my friend to remind him, as gently as possible, the issue was her education and her life—even if he was paying the bills. This good and devoted father was a typical consumer. He knew what he wanted to buy and thought that my school was to provide it.

In addition, consumerism biases the educational process against risk, exploration, and especially against the lessons of failure. This instinct against taking risks influences what our schools advise students to do. We do not urge students to climb too high, lest they fall. Browning's line that one's "reach must exceed his grasp" is fundamental to education, but we become reluctant to advise students to take risks, preferring to measure a student's tasks to offer the best opportunity for success.

When you buy a dishwasher, you know exactly what you want. But education is a journey whose destination cannot be known in advance. We will never know what a student's potential is until the outer limits are tested. Students must leave their safety zones to try things that necessarily present the risk of failure. There is no teacher like trial and error. But consumers do not buy failure, even the risk of failure, and in turn, we are prone to tailor educational advice to what children can safely accomplish. Parents know, in their own cases, the irreplaceable lessons of failure. In an intellectual and academic sense, parents understand failure and its benefits. Yet, they have no such tolerance for failure in the education of their children. Failure and its lessons are not what they are buying.

## Cultural Process and Conflict

Education is a cultural process whereby the skills and requirements for social achievement are transmitted from each generation to the next. There are always, of course, generational conflicts in culture, especially in a culture that prizes personal and political freedom as a basic value.

I want to describe how this cultural and generational conflict expresses itself in contemporary America, and what this conflict means for the purposes of our schools.

In post–World War II America there has emerged a distinctive youth culture—a distinctive subculture having its own fashions and mores, its own distinctive styles, and its particular speech. We do not now perhaps appreciate that this is a quite recent development. Prior to World War II, the word "teenager" did not exist. The word in its present meaning appeared in Webster's in 1961. More importantly, not only did the word not exist, from my own personal experience I can testify that the thing— the animal—did not exist. I was a child of the fifties, and we were not "teenagers." We were apprentice adults. We were in training for the roles that our parents had set for us. No part of childhood permitted us latitude in our ways of thinking and living, and there were no records in our music collection that were for "the children."

Various influences were at work in creating a youth culture. Post–World War II affluence meant that young people became an autonomous consumer group with discretionary income. Madison Avenue had then an immediate and direct interest in creating this market niche because there were distinctive products to be sold to this group of people who, for the first time, had money in their pockets and could choose how to spend it.

Most important was the development of mass media, which spawned an entertainment industry of television, movies, and music, specifically and particularly aimed at the young.

These media were powerful agents of cultural change. Nothing like television, not even the Internet, has happened in my lifetime in terms of transforming the way society organizes itself and how it understands itself. There came to be programs for young people, and a music industry sending the powerful messages of youthful independence which music conveys. If you listen to rock music, you know that the youth culture values indulgence and spontaneity. It does not value the deferred gratification that previous generations were taught so carefully at their mothers' knees. Experimentation with drugs, alcohol, and sex is encouraged. Gratification and gratification "now" are central norms of the youth culture.

I do not recommend that you go to a rock concert, but if you should, think of these events as liturgical celebrations of the youth culture—the ecstatic atmosphere, the music, the lyrics, the dress and, of course, the substance abuse. As a rock concert illustrates, we can understand how basic the cultural conflicts are that our young people must negotiate as they face adulthood. We have a youth culture of indulgence, but the adult legal system imposes a drinking age of 21! The legal requirement is often ignored, but it represents graphically the cultural divide we have created, and the differing norms young people confront when they live among their peers on the one hand and among their parents and teachers on the other.

What I will call the "prevailing adult culture" conflicts with the hedonism and indulgence of the youth culture at almost every point—alcohol and drugs being just cases in point. You and I—our schools—have the unhappy privilege of mediating or arbitrating these disputes since education is the primary vehicle whereby the prevailing norms of the adult culture are imposed on the rising generation. Schools are agents of adulthood being imposed on children. Parents are sometimes with the youth culture and sometimes allies of the schools.

This process of enculturation starts young and takes one of its earliest forms in the parental demand for academic achievement. Parents believe, and the prevailing culture believes, that in an information age, education is the prerequisite for economic success. The cultural assumption is that the exclusive positions in the economic order are at a premium. The elite places are competitively awarded based on academic achievement. School is the essential institution for entry into the adult world.

This belief in the essential need for academic preparation is the primary reason why schools like yours and mine flourish. Good academic preparation opens golden doors, and parents have no higher priority for their children, or for your school and mine, than to see that their children are given the keys to those doors. That requirement carries with it the full weight of adult expectation. Schools and colleges are cultural mediators.

Many parents establish the academic achievements of their children as the single most important measure of their success as parents. Children have daily planners just like the ones that you and I live with, and the elementary years are spent under the watchful supervision of adults from dawn to dusk. A ten-year-old recently told a *Time* reporter that she had no time to be a kid. The days of innocent play and imaginary exploration are at a premium for many children.

A few years ago, I had a serious, intense, and detailed discussion with an alumna about college admission. She was concerned about the most particular details of the process. At some point, I asked her how old her child was. "Four," she replied. This parent is not atypical of her generation. She has extraordinary academic ambitions for her child because she believes such achievement is essential to her child's success. None of this surprises you. You have your own anecdotes at least as telling.

We must see ourselves as mediators in this basic cultural transaction. It is fraught with conflict. The norms of the youth culture are in stark contrast with the assumption that academic success yields an economic reward. Children and schools are caught betwixt and between.

Given this conflict between the norms of the teenage culture and what they are expected to do in school as an introduction to the adult culture, we should not be surprised that adolescents are suffering from stress-related disorders in startling numbers. Suicide is the second leading cause of death among college students. Many students are seeking help for anxiety, depression, eating disorders, and substance abuse. These are significant problems on every American college campus, as I am sure they are at your schools.

Should we be surprised that pills are being dispensed for

so many disorders thought to impair learning? An elementary school teacher told me that she thought she was a pharmacist, not a teacher, because parents are trying to resolve medically any academic handicap their children face. It is not just in Garrison Keillor's *Lake Wobegon* that "all the children are above average."

This cultural tension is a genuinely new thing. In my Alabama hometown it never occurred to me, or to anyone else, that some high school or junior high school failure might permanently mark my future. (I did have the misfortune to have a brilliant older sister who set an academic standard that my parents supposed I should match!) But childhood was a time of freedom and innocence. By contrast, think of all the items on our worry list we are now compelled to warn children about. No wonder they are stressed and distressed. We tell them their world is full of danger.

## Role of Educators

Educators are agents, powerful agents, in this cultural interface. What is it that we should be doing? First, we should be passionate advocates for education understood not as a commodity but as a process of personal growth and intellectual development. We must advocate for education. We must advocate for children. We must advocate for childhood. We should address all our constituencies, all the time, about the purposes of education rightly understood. We must be aggressive in the interpretation and explanation of the academic program in every forum at our disposal.

Wake Forest sends to each entering family a document that we call a "Relationship Covenant" with the request that the family study it together. This covenant describes what Wake Forest offers and provides, and what we require across the domains of campus life and the academic program. We find it helpful to inform our community in advance about our practices and policies.

If these remarks have a cautionary tone, my opinion is that most things in your schools are going very well. You are doing a fine job. This is a most appealing student generation. As a whole, this generation works hard, and they are morally purposeful. You hear complaints about the effort at resume building in high school—the need to appear "well rounded" to colleges—but service learning and other activities are having a dramatic and constructive impact on the way students understand themselves, their world, and their public duties.

Before the collapse of the capital markets, this group of students had already moved on from the 1990s preoccupation with Wall Street and wealth. Programs like Teach for America and the Peace Corps are booming. Many students are doing socially constructive things with their lives after graduation. Idealism is not dead among them. They are hopeful and optimistic, though I venture that the dark lessons of 9/11 have yet to be internalized.

The global outlook is taken seriously by this generation. Wake Forest is one of the schools that retains a foreign language requirement. We once heard complaints about this supposedly outdated degree requirement. No more. More than half of last year's Wake Forest graduating class earned academic credit abroad. There is a serious, thoughtful purpose to master languages so that they can be better prepared to live as citizens of the world.

There are a great many things about this generation to commend. We must continue to alleviate the impact of substance abuse, anxiety, depression, eating disorders, and the other health and safety risks to which young people are exposed. These must remain priority items on our common agenda. We must solicit the thoughtful involvement of parents in these matters. Parents are often ambivalent about drug or alcohol use. They accept substance experimentation as a kind of rite of passage, sometimes without adequate appreciation of the risks involved. None of us fear alcohol as a drug—as we should. Parents often do not know how much more dangerous marijuana has become in the quarter century or so since they may have experimented in college. It is now a dangerous drug with significant psychological and emotional risks.

Parents often favor strict regulation of illegal substances until their own children are involved. Suddenly, they prefer mercy to justice. Much needs to be done to facilitate substantial discussion with parents, teachers, and children regarding these matters. Children receive mixed messages. We must be united as families and schools to limit these risks.

Alcohol abuse by students is first and foremost a concern about well-being and safety. The alcohol culture is entrenched on America's college campuses and has been treated with benign neglect for decades. As you know, however, alcohol use is steadily moving down in age. It is now your problem as well as mine. Neglect of alcohol use is no longer legally or morally acceptable. We are—strangely—much more focused on youth smoking than alcohol use and abuse by children.

The phrase *in loco parentis* is being heard again on America's campuses. In loco parentis must involve not just the issues of drug and alcohol abuse but must reflect a larger concern for the moral and spiritual development of young people. One advantage of private colleges is that we can be intentional and purposeful in the issues of moral and spiritual development which are directly connected to these behavioral and psychological concerns.

## Conclusion

My greatest concern for the best of this generation, the best of your graduates and mine, is that these students are so sophisticated, accomplished, worldly, traveled—perhaps I should say "programmed"—that they have education mastered. They have school figured out. They know where they are going and what it takes to get there. School is a game, and they are the winners. Their parents' dreams are coming true. These are your success stories.

What is missing in this otherwise admirable outlook is any sense of discovery, adventure, wonder, possibility, or any suggestion that they might find around some corner of their minds an unknown passion leading in some new direction. Aristotle said that all knowing begins in wonder, and these most successful of our students lack wonder. They are on the fast track—destinations chosen.

Each year at our convocation for entering students, I recite Shel Silverstein's marvelous little homily, "Magic Carpet." I hope you know it. I trust you will join me in spreading its enduring lesson.

*You have a magic carpet*

*That will whiz you through the air, To Spain or*

*Maine or Africa*

*If you just tell it where.*

*So will you let it take you*

*Where you've never been before,*

*Or will you buy some drapes to match*

*And use it on your floor?*

Too many of our best and brightest students are buying drapes. They have fixed their journey. No matter how much they accomplish or how much they achieve, they may miss the joy and wonder of education as discovery. They may pass up "the ride of their lives."

We must see that the joy and discovery of some domain yet to be explored continues to surprise and delight young minds, for upon such explorations to uncharted territories our future, their futures—indeed the future of the world—depends.

———————————

SOUTHERN ASSOCIATION OF INDEPENDENT SCHOOLS
ATLANTA, GEORGIA (OCTOBER 8, 2002)

# Memorial Service, September 11, 2001, Wait Chapel

Contrary to what you learn from the clock and calendar, our lives do not unfold hour by hour, day by day. Our lives, rather, are marked by events—of celebration and crisis—that are communal and create the common memories that make of us a people, a nation.

The most gripping of these life-marking events are tragic. For all too human reasons, we resist and deny the lessons of the darkness of the soul. The sundial on the old campus spoke for all when it read, "I count only the sunny hours." It takes a catastrophe to overcome our reluctance to accept the lessons of human hate.

Pearl Harbor was that event for my parents' generation. It changed their world, and it changed them forever. They never forgot the moment when the news reached them. For my generation, growing up in the sunshine and optimism of the post-war world, there was the bombing of the 161 Street Baptist Church and the assassinations of Kennedy and King. Each of these events broke my heart and my spirit. My heart and spirit healed, but there are scars that will forever remain.

Now, my dear young friends, you have your generation's day—as Roosevelt said in that immortal phrase— "…that will live in infamy." To your life, experience has added a bitter yet inevitable lesson: there is evil and hatred in the human heart. That lesson will make you sadder. That lesson might also make you wiser.

But the kingdom of the human heart is large. In addition to hate, it contains courage and resolve. In response to the outrage of Pearl Harbor, my father's generation waged and won a great war, then came home to establish a new and more prosperous and just America. You and I inherited the benefits of their courage and their goodness. The ordeal was great and the sacrifice incalculable—visit someday the hallowed beaches and graveyards of Normandy—but prevail they did.

We must now experience shock, grief, disbelief, and anger. It may seem that routine and normal life is out of reach and out of place. But remembering whose children and grandchildren we are, it is time for us to exhibit the character we inherit and resolve to protect and defend the blessings we inherit in this new millennium. Our forebearers did not turn aside, and we must not flinch.

It is likely true that life will now be different and, in many respects, more difficult. The world and travel in it now seem less commonplace, more dangerous. A new kind of war—not fought warrior against warrior but in offices, airports, and apartments—has begun. It is a chilling prospect. But you are America's future. You will not see your promise diminished.

We must pray for President Bush and our national leaders in the making of the grave decisions that are ahead. The welfare of many tribes and kingdoms will depend upon what a few men and women come to believe and decide.

We must be aware also, not only of what terrorism does to America but what we do to America out of fear of it. If we are to be America—free, open, equal under God—we must bear the risks that freedom imposes. We must not, out of fear, become less than the nation whose noble ideals summon our honor and loyalty.

There were moments of epiphany in my undergraduate years when I acquired lessons never lost. I want to share one such moment with you.

Our Shakespeare class was two semesters long. In the first, we studied the comedies, the tragedies in the second. The professor was a man I knew well, having taken several of his courses. In the first session of the second term, he remarked, in an offhand way, that Shakespeare's tragedies were generally regarded as superior works of art to the comedies.

"Why is that?" I asked at once. Mr. Ownby started to reply, but then paused. That pause lengthened into one of those compelling silences, louder than shouts, which seem to last an eternity. The room was utterly still.

Mr. Ownby paced the floor and looked out the window. Finally, he turned to me with an expression on his face that revealed that these were words from his heart and soul: "Because, Mr. Hearn, life is more tragic than comic." There was another pause before the class continued. It was a moment I shall never forget. It is important that you rightly hear what Mr. Ownby told me from his heart. For many years, I mistook his message. He did not say that life is tragic rather than comic. He said life is more tragic than otherwise.

Now, older and perhaps wiser, I know what he meant. We are the sons and daughters of Adam and Eve. Somehow, each generation must learn and relearn the terrible lessons of cruelty, vengeance, and hate.

You will encounter the realities of good and evil, achievement and failure, faith, and despair. The world's story is told in both comedy and tragedy, in laughter and tears. But you must not yourselves be overcome by evil lest you become its agent.

We must recover, and we will. We must resolve to see the triumph of justice, and we will. We must overcome evil and hate with goodness and—pray God—we will.

# The Circles of Character

I am honored to share this occasion with the graduates, staff, families, and friends of the class of 1994 at Woodberry Forest. The ties between Woodberry Forest and Wake Forest University are strong. We share a common last name and much more. I read your history with great interest. Your benefactors and leaders have served my university with great distinction. The names of Hanes, Womble, Gray, Chatham, Bennett, Glenn, Babcock, and Butler have meant a great deal to both of our schools. Over twenty of your recent graduates are on my campus, and eight were prefects. Many of your graduates across the years are ours, and so I have known much of this institution by reputation and personal report. Having been here and in preparation for this occasion, I understand more fully the deep affection and high regard in which Woodberry Forest is held, not only by its graduates but throughout the academic community. You honor me by this invitation, and my wife and I want to express our appreciation to the headmaster and everyone else responsible for making this visit so pleasant and memorable.

A few weeks ago, a group of seniors about to graduate from Wake Forest were at my home for dinner. I asked them if they were to choose a topic for a commencement address for a preparatory school, what that subject should be. One young woman said, without a moment's hesitation, you should talk about character. "Why?" I asked. "It is the most important thing," she said. She is right, and I have taken her advice.

It is a fitting topic for Woodberry Forest. Your honor system is an educational model. The Archer Christian Award is given in part for character. Three recent recipients and senior prefects are at Wake Forest: Will Joyner, Kelly Greene, and John Matthews.

In another life, I was a professor of moral philosophy and taught and wrote on subjects in ethics. At Wake Forest the development of values is one of our institution's most fundamental objectives. I have, therefore, reflected on these matters, both as an academic and as an educator. Moreover, I have watched young people succeed and sometimes fail in the journey you will undertake beyond these walls. In college and in life, it matters what your abilities are. In college and in life, it matters what you know and can do. But in college and in life, it matters most what you stand for, what you are committed to, and the ideals by which your life is governed. Character is destiny.

Commencement is about beginnings. This commencement is about the beginnings of adult life. With adulthood comes life's most difficult and dangerous, yet precious, gift: freedom. You have been taught the ideals of your families and the values of Woodberry Forest. They have been nurtured here in an intense and caring environment. But the values of your family or those of Woodberry Forest do not inevitably become your own. What sort of man will you choose to be? Once you possess the gift of freedom and are free from daily supervision and control, the question that matters is not what or whose controls you are free from, but what will you be free for? The conduct of your life over the next four years will be a major step in how this central issue of your life is to be determined. Since character is destiny, what is yours to be? This question belongs not to your school or your parents. It belongs to every man. It now belongs to you.

In an essay titled "Circles," Ralph Waldo Emerson said, "The life of man is a circle, which, from a ring imperceptibly small, rushes outward in all directions and that without end." I want to talk about the four primary life circles that form your life and constitute character. Character consists in the effective management of your life, and your life consists in, as Emerson said, "a series of ever broadening circles."

## The First Circle

In the center of the circle is, of course, yourself. Character, requires, more than any other asset, the ability to govern your own life effectively. From the development of habits that lead to a healthy body to the deepest issues of self-respect and mental well-being, no issue in life is more fundamental than self-discipline and self-control. The sense of responsibility, which is at the foundation of all life, is the responsibility for self.

While you may worry, and your parents worry for you, about the crime and violence that constitute a risk to your well-being, most of the risks that you encounter in college and in life are self-imposed. The danger and harm most likely to be present on any college campus, or for that matter in any city, will come from your own decisions. Will you use your freedom to experiment with drugs or abuse alcohol? Will you drink and drive or ride in a car with a drinking driver? If you do, and statistics say many of you will, no danger could be greater to your present and future well-being. That is a danger you impose. If you go through college believing that having a good time, being with your friends, overcoming shyness, and feeling accepted involves abusing alcohol, the risks to your future are enormous. The risks and rewards of your life are largely in your own hands.

College campuses are busy places with time demands being made on all sides. No one can manage these demands and establish priorities other than yourself. Most academic difficulties are experienced in the freshman year. Many of these difficulties arise from the abuse of freedom, but almost every academic problem is, at its basis, a problem of time management. Failures of time allocation are failures of self-control. You must manage your life.

The capacity to govern one's own life well, to exercise self-discipline and self-control in responding to the multitude of demands placed upon us, constitutes the foundation of a good life. A prudent and rational ordering of our daily experience is not a natural and inevitable process. We speak too much about the elements of character that regard other people and too little about the difficulties we experience in bringing our own behavior under the control of enlightened self-discipline. The first circle of your character is first in order of priority. Unless you manage your own affairs well, unless you have learned the most difficult discipline, which is self-discipline, the foundation of your life will be uncertain.

Do not abuse the gift of freedom, especially when it is new. Do not experiment with substances and forms of conduct that are deadly. Alcohol is a drug. Abuse it, and it will ruin your life.

## The Second Circle

The second circle of character involves our relationships to those we love and who love us. The first extension of the circle of our lives, and the circle of character, is in relationship to those we love. These associations are the central ingredient in our emotional life. How things are between us and those we love determines the degree and character of our personal happiness more than any other single influence.

In ideal cases, family ties are based in natural love and affection. But as we make the perilous journey from youth to adulthood, conflict and trauma can render family relationships traumatic and difficult. Often these conflicts center around the nature and degree of freedom to be given at the various stages of young manhood. It is important, therefore, that you work effectively at being a son or brother, rather than regarding these relationships as based simply in duty or natural affection. Parent-child relationships must cease as children reach adulthood, but that transition is seldom achieved without difficulty. Work hard to maintain family ties. Where there are difficulties, confront them with your families in honest conversation. You will be amazed at what talk can achieve that quarrel cannot.

It is tragic, but true, that often we show our worst selves to those we love. We are unable to extend to family members the understanding and forgiveness we would readily extend to others. These are difficult and complex issues. Being a good family member is an essential in human welfare.

Learning to be a partner in romantic relationships leading toward the formation of your own families is another crucial task of the years ahead. Sexual relationships contain enormous risk, especially when our personalities are being formed. Concern and responsibility for other people provide the only prospect for a moral relationship between partners. There is all but total confusion about sexual values in our culture. While Sigmund Freud was reviled in his own day for his views about sexuality, the central role that he assigned to the sexual instinct in human social life is now regarded as commonplace. Erotic stimuli are used to sell every product in our marketplace, but codes of personal sexual conduct remain confused and uncertain.

Sexual maturity is among the most difficult achievements of adult life. Our sex education needs to be more candid in recognizing and explaining the difficult task human individuals and societies confront in the control of human sexuality. Concern about AIDS and sexually transmitted diseases gives powerful new emphasis to the demand for honesty among and between sexually active people.

That requirement, too, is more difficult than any of us like to admit. Even people who have been married a long time often cannot communicate easily about sexual matters. In the task of sexual maturity, you will learn how difficult and complex is the task of genuinely loving another person. Love is not easy and natural. Love is a challenge and an awesome responsibility.

Sexual encounters can no longer be casual. A frightening number of this college generation is infected with the AIDS virus. If there is no longer the risk of pregnancy and ruined reputations, as in my youth, there is a greater and more ominous risk of disease and death. The evidence is that alcohol abuse plays a major role in the failure of your age group to practice safe sex. That is another powerful incentive to caution in the use of alcohol.

Some years ago, a beloved friend of my undergraduate days died of AIDS. He was a doctor whose compassion for poor children led him to an inner-city hospital. He was perhaps the best person I have ever known. The world has been robbed of one of its best people. No one is immune from the tragedy of AIDS. You are all at risk, and must join the battle against this killer, beginning with the care of our own body.

There is much too little comment about friendship in human life which forms a major part of this second circle. Friendship is not a necessary and inevitable product of growing up nearby someone. Friends require cultivation and care. No resource of your life is more important or pays such rich dividends.

I have a sister, who having made a friend, never loses touch. She gives an extraordinary effort to remain a friend, and she is always there in good times and bad. Her life is richer for the effort, but her example reminds me that most of us fail in the opportunities and responsibilities of friendship. As you grow older, friends are harder to make and easier to lose. Hang on to your Woodberry Forest friends, wherever your paths take you from today.

## The Third Circle

The third circle of your life requiring the exercise of character concerns public and social life, the values involved in our relationships to political institutions and society at large. Humans gather themselves into societies, share a collective existence, and divide labor among themselves: human groups, not individuals, are self-sufficient. We are all fed, clothed, housed, and cared for by the shared activities of many. Collective life and the division of labor require that social, political, and economic institutions manage these complex interactions among individuals and groups. These institutions regulate our lives to a much greater extent than we commonly notice.

Social life works to the common good of all, but not to the private good of each. The division of labor means that some have better jobs than others and that various positions are assigned creating social and economic inequalities. Society limits your freedom and imposes laws governing almost every aspect of your life. It makes you pay taxes and coerces you to service in the military, even orders you to battle. On D-Day, America sent young men no older than yourselves to die on the beaches of Normandy.

Democratic societies require that individuals choose to undertake the burdens and responsibilities of citizenship. The set of public values that joins this nation is being eroded. We seem increasingly to have lost a sense of personal responsibility for the common good. Instead, we have witnessed the development of an adversarial system of social relationships. On this model, the way to preserve freedom or seek justice is to divide people into special interest groups and have them, literally and figuratively, fight it out. The result of this practice is the alienation of interest groups from each other. More important, it results in the disappearance of the sense of common interest, of the public welfare, and of the general good of the whole. If we are but a collection of warring factions, who speaks for the United States of America? If our society is divided into labor against management, government against business, Blacks against Whites, young against old, we lose collective public beliefs, without which democracy will not long survive.

Many of the most serious questions of human life revolve around the dilemmas of self and society, the individual and others, and personal happiness and the common good. How much personal happiness do you sacrifice for the public gain? Would you have hit the D-Day beaches for the welfare of the nation? By our neglect of the themes of social and public responsibility, colleges and universities are in part responsible for the decline of the commonwealth. Education for citizenship is one of the foundational ideas of liberal education, and this is an ideal we must seek to restore for ourselves and our society.

Surveys of college students indicate a widespread mistrust of public institutions and indifference to public service. Democracy cannot survive without our voluntary commitments to full and effective citizenship. I urge you to embrace responsible citizenship within the circle of your life. Beginning in college, give back as you have been given. Make your college community better because you live there. The Wake Forest Volunteer Service Corps sends students from our campus to serve in almost every agency in Winston-Salem. Next year, our students will build their second Habitat for Humanity house, raising the money and doing the construction themselves. These are vital lessons in citizenship and public responsibility. The United States of America needs your leadership if its values are to flourish in the new century. The nation needs for each one of you to be and to do your absolute best.

## The Fourth Circle

In the surrounding circle of all life are those ultimate commitments involving God and human destiny. Tragically, religion is not inevitably of human benefit. A force so fundamental and powerful is as much abused as a source of blessing. Tune in to any one of several cable channels, and you can see religion at its worst. Throughout history and around the world, we see that the power of religion can be used to nurture hatred as well as love, war as well as peace, division as well as brotherhood.

But misuses do not change the fact that no element in human culture and human nature is more pervasive and fundamental than the religious impulse. God in many forms has spoken through the mouths of many prophets, and each believer, in faith, must, as St. Paul said, "Seek his own salvation with fear and trembling."

It behooves all of us, however, to be reminded that in these matters of the spirit, we walk by faith, not by sight. We need to learn the lessons of humility and tolerance before God—so often absent in believers. As we move to global relationships, the conflicts of various faiths will pose the most difficult world dilemmas. Let us therefore hope that we may believe enough in our God not to demand the imposing on others of our beliefs. We need not substitute our own ideology, whatever it may be, for the divine purpose.

In the search for meaning and faith, we find the self-control to manage our lives, the spirit of love that guides us as families, and the spirit of common life basic to citizenship. Thus, it is in the outer and divine circle that the unity of life is to be found in which we associate the undertakings of our own lives to transcendental and transcendent purpose. St. Augustine said, "God is a circle whose centre was everywhere and its circumference nowhere." Woodberry Forest has given you Christian ideals. There could be no higher wish for its graduates than that this spirit might guide you all the days of your lives.

## Conclusion

A new century will dawn before the class of 1994 has finished your dreaming and begun your doings. What great promise is before you! In the new century we have reason to hope that democratic freedoms will flourish around the world. Former

Congressman and Cabinet Secretary Jack Kemp told the recent Wake Forest graduates that it is 1776 all over the world. So it is. Give yourselves the character to contribute to this era of hope and may God's blessing bring your dreams to vivid fulfillment.

———————————

WOODBERRY FOREST SCHOOL, JUNE 3, 1994

# The Ride of Your Life

Laura and I are honored to be part of this joyful occasion marking this important moment in the lives of all of the Class of 1999 and their families. I have known Westminster primarily through your graduates who have come to Wake Forest University. They have been fine representatives of this school, and I was pleased to meet several of you, at our recent Campus Day, who will be coming in the fall. I have been privileged to know President Clarkson in recent years as a devoted academic leader, and my daughter-in-law, Jennifer Speir Hearn, is a member of your faculty. So it is a personal honor to be part of this celebration.

The longer I live, and the more I experience, the more convinced I am of the truth that nothing is purely good or evil. Each experience in life is a mixture, blessing and curse, risk and opportunity. There is a Chinese parable from the 2nd Century B.C. Taoist Huai-nan Tzu, which Professor Win-Chiat Lee of

Wake Forest's Department of Philosophy, was kind enough to translate for me. It expresses the notion of that mixture, and it provides my theme today:

"Near the border, there once lived a man who was an excellent horseman. One day, without any cause, his horse ran away and entered the neighboring providence of Hu. Everyone expressed sorrow. But his father said, "Why can't this be good fortune?" After a while, the horse returned, accompanied by a second beautiful horse. Congratulations came from everyone. But the father said, "Why can't this be misfortune?" Now with a new fine horse, the son spent much time riding, and he fell and broke his leg. Everyone expressed sorrow. The father said, "Why can't this be good fortune?" After one year, the Hu people invaded the border. Every young man went to war, and nine out of ten died. Yet because of his lameness, the son was spared with his father."

Therefore, the parable concludes, good fortune becomes misfortune and misfortune becomes good fortune. Their mystery cannot be comprehended, and their depth cannot be fathomed. Hence there is a Chinese proverb, "The frontier man lost a horse. How did he know it was not good fortune?"

Hegel's dialectic in Western thought and the Far East notion of Ying and Yang express this notion in philosophical terms. Each thing contains the idea of its opposite, just as love contains the seed of jealousy and anger. Fear can generate courage. Guilt contains the origin of forgiveness and reconciliation. Every blessing, every success, every trait of character contains its opposite and complementary risk. Every failure or disappointment contains the opportunity for learning and growth.

I was recently talking to a Wake Forest coach about an athlete on his team. "How is he doing?" I asked. "Well," he said, "Everything comes easy for him. He is smart, good-looking, and everyone likes him. He is the apple of his parents' eyes, and they do everything for him. He has great talent, but to play at the college level would require a commitment and dedication that he has never been required to make. There is no limit to what he could accomplish if he ever found something that commanded his complete commitment and dedication."

Nothing the coach said was a criticism. He spoke with admiration and affection. But this pattern of easy success contains complementary risks. This is a young man whose potential may never be tested or discovered. He will do well, but might he have the potential for greatness? He may never know. The world may never know.

## The Fortunes of Education

My theme today is education. Those of you graduating are among the fortunate few. In a nation concerned about the quality of secondary education, you have been blessed to attend one of the best schools anywhere. Your academic and developmental needs have been carefully tended to. You have been given careful advice in the face of each decision. Above all, your being at this school reflects your possession of the most important advantage of childhood: the commitment of your families to education and their involvement with your lives.

But let us not forget the parable: might this be misfortune? This wonderful education, this fine school, and the blessings of parental commitment—all primary human goods—contain inevitable risks. Your success in college and, more importantly, in life will depend upon your maximizing the advantages of these opportunities and overcoming the temptations to which these very same blessings expose you.

At this fine school, you have been given opportunities to explore your own abilities and to test the relationship of your skills to the worlds of study, and later, of work. You know which subjects you like and do not like. You know where you succeed and where you struggle. You have become skilled in the arts of academic achievement. You have probably had special learning opportunities. Given these advantages, you are informed, self-aware, savvy, and sophisticated—all the benefits of superior educational opportunity.

Each of these achievements and elements of self-knowledge represent a narrowing of choices, a selection among options. More seriously, these decisions represent assessments of your strengths and ambitions and interests. For you, college may be a fixed transaction, the terms of which you have already mastered. College may be fully realized in your thinking. Indeed, having decided where to go, you may be already thinking past college.

The risks of educational advantage are to preordain education and prescribe your own capacities in relation to learning. We know about college—it is admissions, courses, requirements, credit hours, and for some of you a ticket to graduate and professional school. Or perhaps it is that job opportunity on Wall Street or in Atlanta.

There is, my young friends, all the difference between schooling, going to college, and becoming educated, which is the work of a lifetime. Your education will be a function of the degree to which you are transformed by the experience, discovering new sources and resources of academic and personal growth. You need to seek new academic challenges, new opportunities for service, new moral awareness, and develop religious sensibilities.

Aristotle said that knowledge begins in wonder. Too many ready-made plans are destructive of wonder. Solomon, when he sought from the Lord the gift of wisdom, prayed for a "listening heart"—to listen, to learn, to live in anticipation and expectancy. You, too, must listen to your head and your heart if your life is to be blessed with wisdom.

## Know Where You Stand

In another life, I was a professor of moral philosophy and taught and wrote on subjects in ethics. At Wake Forest, the development of reliable values is our most important institutional objective. I have, therefore, reflected on moral matters, both as an academic and as an educator. Moreover, I have watched young people succeed and sometimes fail in the journey you are able to undertake beyond these walls. In college and in life, it matters what your intellectual abilities are. In college and in life, it matters what you know and what you can do. But in college and in life, it matters most what you stand for, what you are committed to, and the ideals by which your life is governed.

Character is destiny. To be educated is to seek life's highest good—character that bestows upon us the trust of others. In the architecture of values, intelligence is preceded by goodness. The prophet's admonition should be your guide: do justice, love mercy, walk humbly with God.

Some have said that the national moral agony we experienced this year means that character somehow matters less than it should. To the contrary, what this ordeal demonstrates is the calamity that overtakes those—even the great and mighty—who fail to regard the truth as something holy—both in the civil law and in that higher law of God.

With the advent of adulthood comes life's most dangerous and difficult yet precious gift: freedom. You have been taught the ideals of your families and of this school. They have been nurtured in an intense and caring environment. But the values of your family and those of Westminster do not inevitably become your own. What kind of person will you choose to be? Once you possess the gift of freedom and are free from daily supervision and control, the question that matters is not what or whose controls you are free from, but what you are free for?

The conduct of your life over the next four years will be a major step in how this central issue of your life will be determined. Since character is destiny, what is yours to be? This question belongs not to your school or to your families. It belongs to every individual person. This question today becomes yours. I pray that you will seek to cultivate a heart that listens and a mind filled with wonder.

## Stretch to Reach Your Potential

If you are to avoid the temptations that attach to the advantages of your Westminster education, you must be prepared to leave your safety zones, those domains of achievement where you operate with comfort and success. Leaving your safety zone requires that you choose to confront the difficult, the challenging, and the perplexing. You must take courses that allow you to explore the new and unfamiliar.

To stay on the tried-and-true path of preordained outcomes is a notion with all but universal support. But there is no discovery beyond the borders of your potential if you do not take the risk of exploration. Your safety zone is safe, but what lies in that unknown where you have not been?

Your safety zone is perhaps geographic. Traveling to new and unfamiliar places where you had not thought to go can transform your consciousness. A student friend of mine told me that when she called to tell her mother that she was joining that group of Wake Forest students who go to Calcutta each Christmas to care for the dying in Mother Teresa's City of Joy, her mother's reaction was "You want to go where to do what?" But go she did, and she returned with a moral passion that will guide her life henceforth. She left her safety zone. The same person who went to Calcutta did not return.

A Wake Forest student will bike across America this summer to raise awareness and money for breast cancer. Hers is not a trip, not a physical ordeal. It is a pilgrimage.

You know what your safety zones are. To be transformed you must, as Jesus did when he was tempted, take your own pilgrimage into your own desert, and there confront those temptations the mastery over which can offer your life discovery of the fullest measure of your potentiality. Of course, to leave the security of success and achievement exposes all of us to the risks of failure. But as the Taoist parable teaches, many of life's important accomplishments are born in failure. In our errors and mistakes there is growth and opportunity.

As my student friend's mother showed, you cannot expect your parents always to encourage departures from the safety zone. While parents know in general that people learn from failure, they are conditioned to protect you from those difficult lessons in every way possible. In fact, parents spend much of their energy creating your safety zone and attempting to remove every obstacle that might cause you to stumble. But given the freedom that comes with adulthood, there is no option but that you take those risks involved in finding out who you are and what you can accomplish. When you try and fail, think to yourself, "Might this be good fortune?"

A Wake Forest student made a mistake and committed an honor offense. He then committed himself to his own redemption. Now in medical school, he counsels others who have made similar mistakes. His mistake, he says, was his most important blessing. Anna had a serious eating disorder. A misfortune? Yes. But she committed to make her healing the healing of others and led a crusade on our campus that touched many lives.

Emily Dickinson wrote:

> *I dwell in Possibility*
>
> *A fairer House than Prose*
>
> *More numerous of Windows*
>
> *Superior – for Doors*

To explore limits and borders, you must open the windows and doors of possibility, of creativity. There is perhaps too much emphasis in education on those topics where there are prescribed answers to fixed problems to which we must be intellectually subservient. But in the world of the imagination, you, individually, bring to the world unique objects of your own choosing and making.

The fine and performing arts are sometimes represented as if they are merely sophisticated forms of entertainment. But the arts are deeply educational and create in us the disposition to contribute something original and unique. So spend time in the years ahead in the company of artists, musicians, poets, writers, and performers.

Now that you know you should have kept taking violin or piano or art lessons, college is the time to give your creativity its full expression. Einstein is reported to have conceived the theory of relativity when he decided one day to imagine what it would be like to ride on a beam of light.

Many, perhaps most, successful students come to college for schooling and for degrees. Ironically since they know so much, they expect too little, and too little is achieved. The basis of the kind of education that transforms is that you discover and pursue a dream for your life, that you find a calling that gives energy and passion to your study and secures the basis for a meaningful life.

In the end, education is about dreams. Through education our dreams are given the form of ambition, and we achieve the skills and capacity to make of our ambitions the substance of our lives. Dreams, born in wonder and imagination, give our lives passion and commitment.

Dreams are, by their nature, ephemeral and often unrealistic as measured by the safety zones we have established. Find your dream, do something that no one, not even yourself, believes that you can accomplish. Make Westminster and its rich heritage the basis of a broadening vision of what your life can become.

The prophet Joel said that the Lord would pour out his spirit on the people and the young men and women would dream dreams and see visions. Some blessed few of you perhaps have a dream and the ambitions that dreams engender. But most of us must be seekers. Some of us give up too soon. To be or to do something remarkable and creative begins with a vision.

Do not merely go to college and get a degree and then a job. Pursue your dream. In that pursuit, you will discover your greatest personal potential and your most unique and remarkable contribution to the world. In becoming a Big Brother at Wake Forest, Mark realized that friendship was not enough to save at-risk children. So he is an inner-city teacher who has created a coalition of support to take disadvantaged children all the way to college. Mark has a dream; the dream has given his life passion and purpose. I have come to love one of those children's homilies by Shel Silverstein called "Magic Carpet." It contains my gift of words for you on this day of anticipation and hope.

> *You have a magic carpet*
> *That will whiz you through the air,*
> *To Spain or Maine or Africa*
> *If you just tell it where.*
> *So will you let it take you*
> *Where you've never been before,*
> *Or will you buy some drapes to match*
> *And use it on your floor?*

Your magic carpet is, of course, your imagination and your education. This carpet can take you to remarkable and wonderful places. If you decide just to go to school and get a degree— remaining secure within your circle of safety—you have chosen to put your carpet on the floor. The magic is gone. All that remains is for you to hang the drapes.

But your carpet can take you, if you choose, from Westminster to college and beyond on miraculous journeys whizzing through the air in pursuit of wondrous dreams and extraordinary deeds. Do not miss this ride. For this is the ride of your life.

---

COMMENCEMENT ADDRESS AT THE WESTMINSTER
SCHOOLS, ATLANTA, GEORGIA (MAY 22, 1999)